Verner,
may this book
enrich your life....
love & light,
Nadia

THE
CHRONICLES
OF
NADIA

AN INSPIRATIONAL GUIDE TO TRUTH, VITALITY, AND SPIRITUALITY

NADIA ROCHELLE

Contents

Foreword

BY JOHN-PAUL MOORE

Have you ever met someone for the first time and had the immediate gut feeling that you knew this person? You know you've never met, but you have to intentionally convince yourself of the fact that this is a first-time encounter? It's an incredible feeling that resonates throughout every embrace, every meeting of the eyes, and every conversation. You begin to laugh in tandem or surprisingly finish each other's sentences. You lean on the other and think, "Finally, someone is here to catch me." At times it's tempting to ask that person, "Where have you been hiding?" But then it occurs to you that they were never hiding. It's like the myth of the pot of gold at the end of the rainbow. They were shining their bright and beautifully colored light your way and you finally reached the source. The only difference is there's no leprechaun guarding the treasure. The treasure you encounter has a worth that cannot be quantified. It can only be experienced, appreciated, and cherished. That was the feeling that overwhelmed me when I first met my dear sister whom I affectionately call my "twin," Nadia Perry.

I had heard of Nadia several times through our mutual friend, DeWayne Wallace. He often compared us to each other and I would laugh it off in stride. I just knew there would be no way we could be as identical as he described. But once we finally met, it was magnetic. The parallels were dumbfounding. Simple tangible similarities such as a lady bug key that I've never seen anyone have before, but my beloved Nadia had the exact same one. Then there were the headphones by Bob Marley that "magically" we both attentively enjoy our music through. They might as well have been a his-and-her set.

Beyond those accessories, we both mourn the loss of a beloved sibling, Nadia's brother, Lance and my sister, Blendale Alisha. We also cerebrate the lives of our paternals: Nadia's Tolliver "Doc" Percell Perry and my Rev. Robert Lee Moore, Sr. We also cherish our mothers, Wilodean and Blendale. Not to mention the way we love on our siblings, nephews, and nieces, our similar childhood upbringing in the church, our family values, our spiritual journey to embrace our individuality, our love for travel, and so much more we will continue to discover. We find ourselves reflecting the love in each other in so many ways that I can say I truly owe DeWayne his props. He knew emphatically that we would be "two peas in a pod."

Throughout the seven years that we've been blessed to enjoy this journey together, Nadia and I have been beacons of light for each other. Whether it was road trips to the cabins or Chicago, Facetime calls in the wee hours of the night, pop-up visits in New York, or laughs over dinner and drinks, we've effortlessly found ourselves present in each other's corner and by each other's side. We partner on projects through my branding firm, JP Designs Art as Nadia supports our clients as a Creative Consultant. I love to have Nadia on our consultation calls because my confidence in her powerful ability to tap into our clients' vision and elevate it to levels unknown is certain. I am so proud of the mind-blowing creative and visionary that Nadia has revealed herself to be. Nadia is a force that I believe the half has yet to be told.

I remember the first time I saw Nadia perform and she OWNED the stage. Her ability to sing, act, dance, and write revealed layers of magnificent talent, skill, and anointing that literally brings me to tears. There in that theater at Morehouse College I balled my eyes out. I was overjoyed to see my "twin" living in a moment of her manifested dream. We all knew it was in her and finally the universe was her audience. There are some stars, but to me, Nadia is a galaxy all her own.

I can hear Nadia say, "It is not BY me, it's only THROUGH me." Through Nadia, several lights have been turned on in my life that have brought clarity, peace, and a joy that I find incomparable. Phrases she's shared with me, such as, "Gratitude brings abundance" have transformed my perspective in life. This phrase has caused gratitude to be a lifestyle that I live and I welcome all of its benefits. Other affirmations she has shared with me like, "I am committed to living a life I love" cause me to pause and consider what truly matters in life. I can also hear Nadia saying, "Everything is as it should be, only your response must change." This call to surrender has brought such ease to how I address challenges and illusions of failures in my life.

I often call Nadia the modern-day Harriet Tubman because she has the trailblazing power to liberate the mentally enslaved and incarcerated. Ms. Tubman said,

"Every great dream begins with a dreamer. Always remember, you have within you the strength, the patience, and the passion to reach for the stars to change the world. I freed a thousand slaves, and I could have freed a thousand more if only they knew they were slaves."

What courage it takes to find your freedom and go back to free the others. What bravery blossoms in someone who finds the light at the end of the tunnel and dares to call others out of darkness. Ms. Tubman could have been content in a life without shackles, but she thought enough to dismantle the cycle of slavery for her beloved.

Throughout The Chronicles of Nadia, you will discover there are shackles you didn't know needed to be broken. It won't be pretty and in fact it may even be painful at times to address these shackles. But I encourage you to surrender the need to control the narrative of how this book will transform your life. Allow yourself to immerse in the possibility that you are love and deserve to be loved by yourself and others. The freedom you will find may be one you never imagined was possible. You can have freedom from self-hurt, unforgiveness, fear, failure, pride, judgement, and so much more.

Take the time to experience, appreciate, and cherish the journey of The Chronicles of Nadia because there are miraculous moments of liberation, self-awareness, and transformation waiting for you.

Prologue

Being present to yourself is the beginning
of a journey without end

— **ROGER HOUSDEN**

Once upon a time, I stood off in the distance in the background of my life, watching it all happen. I screamed my name to give direction, but I never heard myself. I was too preoccupied with my lack of consciousness. I walked from room to room, door to door, job to job, friend to friend, and lover to lover. I was a lost soul feeling around in the dark. I called out to my heart but it couldn't hear me amidst the clutter and clamor that sang loudly. My spirit and my mind started an unending war. My soul cried aloud to interrupt the battle, but I never recognized the sound of peace that was beckoning me back to the shore.

As I looked out onto my life from the emotional abyss, I wondered, "How will I surrender?" It seemed as if I were too far gone to reel my life to the nearest lighthouse. The dark clouds are more present than ever as they hover at every turn. How do I return myself to myself? How will I wake up my consciousness? Who will turn on the light for me? I can't remain as a prisoner of my own life. Oh to be present again! I must go and grow lest I die.

But, wait!

Is that the sun I feel kissing the broadness of my forehead?

It is so familiar but so new.

As I take in its warmth, I am refreshed and RENEWED!

A miracle is taking place NOW.

If only I knew sooner that my miracle was as simple as choosing it. My former choices aren't pleased with my transformation of mind. I'm aware of my power now. I am choosing to let my darkness die to my light. I feel awakened, fully present, fully illuminated, fully aware of who I am, and what I AM here to do. I'm a light in darkness and I'll show you The Way.

I was once that girl who accepted mediocrity because I didn't know my worth. Recognizing that truth has led me to the understanding that I'm by no means mediocre; mediocrity is simply what I chose. Acknowledging that truth is a vital part of my journey to Queendom. I forgive myself for not always choosing what best serves me. I now acknowledge all of my poor decisions as teachers. I don't hold myself hostage to any guilt associated with choices that I made out of ignorance, resistance, or defiance. The present moment is now my daily gift.

Today, I recognize my value as a QUEEN.

I love myself.

I honor myself.

I respect myself.

I accept myself as I Am.

**Today, I know that I Am worth it,
I deserve it, and I Am Enough.**

Introduction

Growing up as a Southern girl who lived in the Bible Belt, going to church was a regular occurrence. Living an upstanding Christian life was indeed the standard set before me. I mean, what other options did I have? Well, that's not how I sincerely believe that should happen. However, that's typically how it plays out. Whatever the faith is that your family practices, you just inherit it, right? And you take on all of the other cultural influences of their version of that religious practice. You emulate the way they pray, praise, worship, or read their Bible. This is definitely how I acquired my spiritual foundation and I'm forever grateful for it. This foundation has given me a lot to build on. I've always had a thirst, a hunger, and a zeal for more knowledge of God.

But after a period of time I began to feel stuck. Going to church regularly just wasn't satisfying enough. I had memorized scriptures from hearing them repetitively in church services, but as a lad, I had no real idea what a lot of it meant. I started seeking for more understanding. I asked more questions than the normal kid in church. I would pick up the Bible, but I didn't know where to begin and I certainly didn't comprehend the language. Eventually, a woman came into my life as a Godsend when I was a teenager. She became my literal godmother. She was so knowledgeable and learned about the scriptures. I asked her how to study the bible and then began the blossoming of my personal relationship with God and my individual spiritual growth. She helped to equip me with tools to help me study the Bible and pray the "word of God." I was excited to know more and grow more. The eyes of my understanding were opened to a great degree.

As I grew in chronological maturity, quite naturally my curiosity broadened. I longed to know more. I had questions. Questions that needed answering, not pacifying. Questions that dug beyond the surface things I'd heard, seen or experienced. Questions that tradition couldn't satiate any longer. I was seeking for a truth that no one else's journey could give to me. Not my mom's, my pastor's, nor my church friends' journeys. I had studied the Bible, gone to seminary for a stint, and had in-depth conversations with some of the most profound Bible scholars. But I knew there was more and I now know there always WILL BE more! I have traveled a few places around the globe and conversed with people of various backgrounds, cultures, religious practices, and schools of thought. I'm talking about people whose views differ drastically from my foundation. But I find that there's always a common ground— LOVE!

Each time I have the privilege of exchanging thoughts and ideas with diverse beings, I walk away with my mind expanded, enlightened and awakened to truths that resonate with me no matter how different we are. Each time—I GROW! What I know is this—we are all seeking to find our own truth, and it's not in one specific location or aggregation of people. I've found that the only way to keep growing spiritually is to be willing to learn something from every person you encounter on your path EVEN IF it's not what you've been previously taught or told. I'm continuously growing because I'm ever learning from everyone around me. I realize that tradition isn't the only way to learn, but it is a surefire way to stay comfortable, limited, and boxed in. I'd venture to say experience is sometimes a much better teacher! The only way to grow is to embrace change and remain teachable. If you're afraid to expand what you know, then you're afraid to grow.

As you turn these pages, it is possible that your current state of being will be challenged. You may even feel uncomfortable at times with how a particular entity is regarded or approached. The unfamiliar can be off-putting but be compassionate to yourself as you dare to enlighten yourself and stretch your cognition beyond its familiar boundaries. Give yourself permission to grow. Remember to breathe! It's the only way you can stay present and clearly hear your thoughts.

Disclaimer: The intent of these writings is to spur the reader onward towards his or her greatest self. The approach is also intended to be universal so as to reach a broader audience. In keeping with that universal approach, it would be appropriate to use gender-neutral terms in some instances. However, the gender-neutral terms can sometimes add confusion to the overall message. So in an effort to ensure an "easy read," at points I will use "he," "him," and "his" to refer to God or mankind in general. In no way am I disregarding the Divine Feminine characteristics of humanity or the Godhead. In addition, my interchangeable use of Creator, Spirit, Love, Spirit of Love, Universe, Source, and the Divine is with respect to the various aspects of God and is meant to include the perspective of all spirit beings.

Part One:

THE SELF-LOVE CHRONICLES

Self-Love Chronicle, No. 1

LOVE CODES, PART 1:
THE RESPONSIBILITY OF SELF-LOVE

When we expand our thinking and beliefs our love flows freely. When we contract we shut ourselves off. Can you remember the last time you were in love? Your heart went 'Ahhh'! It was such a wonderful feeling. It is the same with loving yourself except that you will never leave once you have your love for yourself. It's with you for the rest of your life, so you want to make it the best relationship you can have.

— LOUISE L. HAY

TODAY'S CHRONICLE FROM NADIA

My dearest love,

Sometimes we blame others for not being everything we need. We have so many trust issues that we are blocking love from flowing to us because we have decided how others should show us love. We can be so blinded by fear, resentment, and anger that we don't even recognize when we are being loved. We find it easier to criticize and fix our significant others, companions, life partners, and friends than to deal honestly with our own issues.

We all started out as love beings. No one came into being inherently angry, resentful, hurt, bitter, fearful, or untrusting. Life happened to you and you closed the womb of your love. Now love can't flow out and it can't flow in. Doesn't that make you tired, exhausted, heavy, and unfulfilled? The truth is you weren't designed to be a nest egg of negativity, harboring all of the unloving attributes there are in your own little shell of safety. Living your life in resistance to who and what you are is a pretty miserable existence.

Whose responsibility is it to reactivate your power of love? No one owes you anything. You chose resistance and you have that same power to choose love again. To make your spouse, partner, parents, siblings, children, pastors, religious leaders, and friends responsible for giving you what you won't give to yourself is completely unfair! If YOU love you, you will attract love TO you. We were created in love, to love, for love, with love to be love. Contrary to what we have subscribed to as truth, love isn't an emotion. It is a state of being. No one else can BE it for you. Take responsibility for your state of being. As long as we keep thinking that there is anything higher than Love, we will be on an endless search to find what we already are and what we always have been. Get back to the original YOU. Be who you were created to be! Be LOVE!

With Infinitely Unconditional Love,

TODAY'S THOUGHT:

*I found that there is only one
thing that heals every problem
and that is to love yourself.*

— LOUISE HAY

TODAY'S SELF-LOVE JOURNAL

Today, I found it challenging to love myself when

_____

_____

_____

_____

Today, I found it easy to love myself when

_____

_____

_____

_____

The key thought from Today's Chronicle I will focus on is

_____

_____

_____

_____

Self-Love Chronicle No. 2

LOVE CODE PART 2: MAINTAIN YOUR POWER

My Dearest Love,

Although it cannot be qualified or quantified, and is formless, Love can take shape. You can mold it as you wish. Love has dimensions. One of the important aspects in the mathematics of love is space. Who or what do we allow into our intimate places? And how often? Again, everyone is made from love, with love, and for love by the Creator. However, all too often, we are looking outside of ourselves for something that we already are. Can you imagine how frustrating that must be to walk around in constant fear of not being loved? How can you expect someone to give you what you won't first give to yourself? That very fear is the breeding ground for the negative toxins that have some of us lost and buried in the mental and even physical weight we carry.

Once you are aware of yourself as a love being and you are doing your due diligence in keeping yourself "in shape," will you continue to allow yourself to be disfigured by the darkness of someone else's lack of consciousness or will you choose to let your light penetrate the darkness? When you understand the far-reaching effects of the light of love, then you realize that you don't have to be in close proximity for it to be effective. Sometimes the best way to demonstrate love is to continue being supportive and caring to someone while giving them the space they need to sit with themselves. When you make an investment in the qualities of life that are invaluable, you hold on to them at whatever cost. You cannot afford to readily hand those precious gems over to things, people, or circumstances that are in no way worth it. We like to think that someone or something takes our power from us. But if we were to be completely honest with ourselves, we give it away senselessly. Keep this in mind: If it doesn't edify, if it isn't yielding a bountiful return, if it isn't positively shaping and impacting your being, you simply have to be unwilling to show up and participate. That, my companions, is how you maintain your peace, joy, love, and light.

With Infinitely Unconditional Love,

TODAY'S THOUGHT:

*I found that there is only one
thing that heals every problem
and that is to love yourself.*

— LOUISE HAY

TODAY'S SELF-LOVE JOURNAL

Today, I found it challenging to love myself when

_____

_____

_____

_____

Today, I found it easy to love myself when

_____

_____

_____

_____

The key thought from Today's Chronicle I will focus on is

_____

_____

_____

_____

Self-Love Chronicle, No. 3

LEARNING LOVE'S LANGUAGE

TODAY'S CHRONICLE FROM NADIA

Dear Lover,

Have you ever heard the phrase, "When in Rome, do as the Romans do?" Well, wouldn't that include speaking the language? Whatever your native tongue, when you go to another country where your language isn't widely spoken, you will likely have difficulty communicating with the people who live there. Not being able to speak the language would probably hinder your ability to navigate freely and enjoy your experience.

With that said, what IS the language of Rome? If you said Romanian, you're wrong! You might have ASSUMED that was correct based on the name of the country. Romanian, however, is spoken in Romania. Rome, on the other hand, is in Italy; therefore the language of Rome is Italian. Now let's assume that LOVE is a huge country and that its citizens are called LOVERS and let's apply the same philosophy to it.

When in LOVE, do as Lovers do! In order to navigate in Love and get the best experience while there, it is imperative that you learn the language. By all means, don't assume that you know what the language is. Take the time to learn what language is spoken there. It may not be the same language you speak and have spoken easily your whole life. It worked for you in YOUR country, but it won't work in THIS place called Love. You keep trying to figure out why you can't get past a certain point with the Lovers in Love. You're frustrated with why you don't have access to certain things, and why you aren't getting the most out of your experience there, right? It's because you're a foreigner and you're walking around Love like a tourist.

You researched places to go and things to do. You got your passport to allow you into the country. You checked out the weather. You learned about the food you wanted to eat. You booked your flight and you went into Love not really knowing how long you would stay. So, you didn't learn any of the language. Sure, the people are nice and some of the Lovers speak your native language. That will help you out for a little while. But if you're planning to stay for any length of time, you can't operate as a tourist forever.

For some of us Love can be a foreign land. We aren't well traveled in it; we have never been outside of the comfort of our own "country." Our way is the only way there is because it's all we know. In my opinion, an un-teachable heart is of the worst kind there is. It has no desire to open up and expand. It only wants to release what limited experience it has and impose it on others. I recently learned by taking The Love Language test by Dr. Gary Chapman that I have three love languages I respond to. Ironically, I can also communicate in English, Spanish, and Thai, with English being my native tongue. Why do I know languages other than my native tongue? It's because I'm an eternal student and I want to learn how to communicate with as many people as possible.

As the saying goes, you should "Broaden your horizons and step outside of the box." Get out of your comfort zone and become a student of your Lover's language. It will help you get better acquainted with the culture of your lover's love. You don't HAVE to learn your lover's language, but it will make for a better stay in the Land of Love if you do. These are the very same suggestions made to people who travel abroad. I want to suggest that you just be open to expanding your limited understanding of Love altogether, even in the most non-romantic sense. Just like there's more to the world than the few places you've traveled, there's more to Love than your limited experiences. As Pastor Greg Stamper affirmed in his "Free To Love" teaching from his sermon series "Love is the Message," "I loose Love from all I thought it was and I go FREE!!" Love is too vast a country to be limited to your "travel" experience.

To gain your citizenship in Love and be recognized as an authentic Lover, learn the language. No one is trying to take away your original language! After all, what's wrong with being bilingual?

In the spirit of love,

Nadia

TODAY'S THOUGHT

Learn eternally. Be a student of love!
Expand yourself as Love! Be free to love!

TODAY'S LOVE LANGUAGE JOURNAL

Today, I found it challenging to speak lovingly to myself when

_____

_____

_____

_____

Today, I found it easy to speak lovingly to myself when

_____

_____

_____

_____

The key thought from Today's Chronicle I will focus on is

_____

_____

_____

_____

Self-Love Chronicle, No. 4

JUMPSTARTING YOUR SPIRITUAL DEVOTION

TODAY'S CHRONICLE FROM NADIA

My Sweetest Beloved,

I remember vividly being a teenager and having this yearning to know more about God than what I had been getting in my Sunday morning experience. I would often pick up my King James Version of the Bible, but I had no idea where to begin. I thought, "Hey! I'll start at the beginning!" So I started at Genesis and, needless to say, I understood very little as I read through the entire Pentateuch (first five books of the Bible). I quickly became discouraged, and I wouldn't pick it back up for days at a time. But the one thing I was certainly familiar with was prayer. I had seen and heard my mother pray devoutly, and there was ALWAYS prayer going on at church. There were phrases I had heard others say while praying that I memorized and mimicked. I initially kept it kind of simple. I felt like I was feeling around in the dark, trying to find my way. And eventually I did!

I learned several things as I kept trying to find my path of spiritual devotion. I learned that everyone's spiritual path is personal, individual, and internal with God within first. There is no set formula for your time of solitude with God. As with any new relationship that is being built, there must be regular communication and quality time spent. It is important to intentionally devote some uninterrupted, non-preoccupied time for just you and Spirit. If you draw close to Him, He'll draw close to you! I've also learned that the closer you draw to Him, the more He reveals Himself. And the more you learn of Him, the more you learn of YOU. Beyond even the learning there is a FEELING of connection. Pastor Yolanda Batts says it this way: "God is not an intellectual exercise, rather, God is a FELT reality." I've learned that praying affirmatively, reading spiritual and inspirational literature, meditating, burning incense, and singing, playing, and listening to songs of worship, love and adoration are vital components in my building an intimate environment and close-knit relationship to God.

From my own experience, I realized that being a new student of the Bible can be difficult. So if reading the Bible interests you, I'd recommend you start out with a New International Version (NIV) Study Bible that includes a commentary to explain each verse. In the Old Testament, it may be helpful to read Psalms and Proverbs during your time of devotion. In the New Testament, you may find that there is MUCH to feed your soul in the Gospels (Matthew, Mark, Luke, John) and the Epistles (The letters from Apostle Paul starting with the book of Romans).

You can also enhance your spiritual practice by keeping a journal, using prayer books, and reading daily devotional materials and other empowering, inspirational, informative texts. If you are of another faith and need help navigating through a particular book or religious literature, don't be afraid to ask a brother or sister of your faith for guidance that will develop your understanding.

I've also learned the importance of having spiritual guidance from a fellow believer who may be more mature or advanced in their spiritual journey. This person could be a priest, pastor, minister, church member, co-laborer, co-worker, friend, family member, life partner, or mentor. You'll typically be drawn to them and them to you! As you pray, meditate, or think positively, ask The Spirit to send that person in your path and give you the discernment to recognize them when they come. Don't try to hold them hostage when they come into your life. It may only be for a season to help you grow. Their presence in your life should not crutch, cripple, or coddle you. As you mature, at some point you, too, may be the answer to someone's prayer for a spiritual guide.

Enjoying the journey,

Nadia

TODAY'S THOUGHT

I want to grow authentically and take my rightful path so that I continuously evolve as my highest self.

TODAY'S SPIRITUAL DEVOTION JOURNAL

Today, I found it challenging to focus on my spiritual devotion

when_____

_____

_____

_____

Today, I found it easy to focus on my spiritual devotion when

_____

_____

_____

_____

The key thought from Today's Chronicle I will focus on is

_____

_____

_____

_____

Self-Love Chronicle, No. 5

DAILY MERCY

Great is thy faithfulness!! Great is thy faithfulness!! Morning by morning new mercies I see! All I have needed your hands have provided. Great is thy faithfulness Lord unto me!

TODAY'S CHRONICLE FROM NADIA

Dear You,

This hymn is one of my favorites simply because it reminds me that God is All Compassion. No not "all compassionate" like a personality trait. God isn't a human with personalities, attitudes, feelings and emotions that changes Its mind about Its perfect creation. God isn't a moody narcissist that withdraws Itself from you if you don't do what it wants you to do. God is not a tyrant, waiting to exact Its punishment on you to keep you under Its control and dictatorship. God is Loving Energy, Breath, Spirit, Prana, Ki, Chi, Shapeless Substance. God is ALL. And God is operating THROUGH all.

This hymn is derived from the scripture Lamentations 3:23 (KJV) which states, "It is of the Lord's mercies that we are not consumed, because his compassions fail not. They are new every morning: great is thy faithfulness.

You see here that "mercies" and compassions are basically used interchangeably. The word for "mercy" in Greek is "eleos," meaning mercy or compassion. Now, in the first verse of this hymn you see a picture of the essence of God as All Compassion being beautifully delineated:

"Great is thy faithfulness, oh God my Father! There is no shadow of turning with Thee. Thou changest not, thy compassions they fail not! As thou hast been and forever wilt be."

Here we see a Loving Source that isn't fickle and doesn't change His/Her mind about you regardless of the decision you make. It has nothing to do with forgiveness from this God that hadn't changed His/Her mind about you. God isn't condemning you so God has no need to forgive you. It's about YOU having an opportunity to choose liberally even if poorly so, realize it, learn from it, grow from it, let it go, forgive YOURSELF for how YOU changed your mind about you.. and making a new choice in the very next moment. Call that moment morning, call it new light, call it the next breath...just know you can choose again. You can choose differently, more wisely, better and then foolishly again and Love won't fail. God won't fail. All Compassion won't fail. What a Loving Source to have considered how important it is to one's growth to be restored Moment by moment, awareness by awareness, breath by breath, enlightenment to enlightenment, awakening to awakening (morning by morning). I wonder what would happen if we patterned ourselves after this blueprint? What if we never figuratively zipped off our cloak of love in exchange for a garment of judgment? What if we realized that people respond better to love than to punishment? ...ourselves included? As a Course in Miracles teaches: Mistakes are for correction...not punishment (paraphrased). "Every mistake must be a call for love." Essentially, Love is the only appropriate response to error or mistake.

No matter the occurrence, make up your mind to be merciful, loving, forgiving, understanding, patient with, and compassionate to yourself and others as you learn, grow and correct your mistakes. Let yourself ever expand as a container, a vessel, a host, a home for Love. Let All Compassion flow through you. Don't let your love fail!

With unfailing love for you,

Nadia

TODAY'S THOUGHT

It is of the Lord's mercies that we are not consumed, because his compassions fail not. They are new every morning: great is thy faithfulness.

– LAMENTATIONS 3: 22-23 (KJV)

I freely give mercy away because it is freely given to me!

TODAY'S DAILY MERCY JOURNAL

Today, I found it challenging to accept God's daily mercy when

_____

_____

_____

_____

Today, I found it easy to accept God's daily mercy when

_____

_____

_____

_____

The key thought from Today's Chronicle I will focus on is

_____

_____

_____

_____

Self-Love Chronicle, No. 6

OVERCOMING LONELINESS: THE LOVE MIND VERSUS THE FEAR MIND

TODAY'S CHRONICLE FROM NADIA

Dear Love Bug,

There is something interesting about the human brain. Although it stores an absurd amount of information, it doesn't exactly file it for you in certain compartments. You have to choose how to categorize the information as it enters your mental hard drive. You have to decide if it's real or fake, true or untrue, or fact or fiction.   We attend motivational, spiritual, or religious gatherings and hear truths about the respective written texts from our life coaches, pastors, leaders, or spiritual teachers. We read these texts and absorb the written information presented there. We hold it as the truth. But the moment a life event happens that challenges what we chose to believe, our truth is shaken. Our truth might even be devalued by our behavior, which suggests that we never really digested that truth. We often abandon our truths for the lies stored by our adversary, enemy and faithful archrival—FEAR!

The moment our mental enemy realizes our foundation is shaken and our defenses are down, it goes in for the kill! It isolates us so we can be alone with our thoughts of failure, defeat, hurt, and disappointments. Fear convinces us that no one understands, no one cares, no one can relate, and no one is there for us. This can only be true when you CHOOSE to believe it. But where is the evidence to support fear as truth? The truth is it's only as real as you empower it to be. The very same mind you used to fortify fear is the same mind you use to fortify loving and empowering truths. You simply need to renew your divine truths. They aren't out of your reach. They are as close as your loving mind. They are as close as your next breath.

Here's the loving truth—you're NEVER alone. You aren't worthless. You won't fail. There is NOTHING too hard for God—not even YOU!   While our opposing, fearful mind convinces us to isolate ourselves in a way that can disconnect us from our spiritual strength, God, on the other hand, is patiently waiting for us to return to the truth that nothing you have done, can do, will do, or may be doing right now will cause Love to leave you alone and helpless without a way out! That is the benefit of Source's all encompassing, unending, unconditional LOVE!

Come out of seclusion and illusion. Abandon the lies of the mind that incapacitates you and wants nothing good for you. Stand guard at the door of your mind. Reject what doesn't serve you well and make room for all that brings you solitude. YOU are the gatekeeper of your own peace!

In Friendship,

TODAY'S THOUGHT:

I'm here. I love you. I don't care if you need to stay up crying all night long. I will stay with you. There's nothing you can ever do to lose my love. I will protect you until you die, and after your death I will still protect you. I am stronger than Depression and I am braver than Loneliness and nothing will ever exhaust me.

— FROM EAT, PRAY, LOVE BY ELIZABETH GILBERT

No matter what it looks like or feels like, I am NEVER alone! I am worthy of living a life of loving peace.

TODAY'S OVERCOMING LONELINESS JOURNAL

Today, I found it challenging to overcome loneliness when

_____

_____

_____

_____

Today, I found it easy to overcome loneliness when

_____

_____

_____

_____

The key thought from Today's Chronicle I will focus on is

_____

_____

_____

_____

Self-Love Chronicle, No. 7

DEPRESSION DOESN'T DISCRIMINATE

TODAY'S CHRONICLE FROM NADIA

My Peace-Filled Love,

No illness that I've ever heard of takes the time to reason out who it will strike. Not cancer, not lupus, not asthma, not eczema, not blindness, not HIV/AIDS, not cerebral palsy, not sickle cell, not multiple sclerosis, not food allergies—not even DEPRESSION! Depression doesn't only affect people in poverty or low socioeconomic status. It is not just attracted to the homeless or people in the hood. It doesn't care how much money you have made, how many degrees you have, what designer clothes you wear, the mansion you live in, or the car you drive. Just in case you thought you could be exempt by making more money, paying off all your debt, getting some well-to-do friends, earning your doctorate degree, pastoring a mega church, or meeting the man or woman of your dreams--let me be the first to interrupt that fairytale for you. IT'S ALL A HORRIBLE LIE.

Depression is a mood disorder and it is most often considered a mental illness that affects one's day-to-day functions in various ways. It can impact ANYONE! It can show up as severe feelings of hopelessness, helplessness, lethargy, and changes in eating habits and weight, or a lack of drive or motivation. It can affect how you think, physically feel, behave, and interact with others. Many factors have been cited as the cause of depression, such as genetic predisposition, neurological and chemical changes in the body, childhood trauma, death of a loved one, life trauma of varied sorts, and the mundane stresses of daily life. Some of us are so conditioned to hoarding stress that we are completely unaware that we are in a depressed state. In fact, the adrenaline and cortisol released by stress can develop in us an addiction to the craving of the sensation that stimulates us into a high of sorts. In other words, even if we experience momentary peace or relief, it is so unfamiliar to us that we will unknowingly find stressful thoughts or create stressful situations to give us our fix.

Depression shows up as an outward expression of an internal conflict. Depression can happen when we unknowingly develop an addiction to stress.

In his book "Becoming Supernatural," Dr. Joe Dispenza beautifully delineates the picture of stress addiction that morphs into depression and he informs us that "living in stress is living in survival." He takes us on a journey of severe illness to supernatural recovery in the life of a woman named Anna whose husband committed suicide, resulting in Anna's emotional trauma that caused her to live from survival mode. He notes that while we are all wired to deal with short-term spurts of stress, no organism can continue living in "emergency mode" for extensive amounts of time without adverse effects.

He connotes how Anna daily relived the events of her husband's suicide and that her body could not differentiate between the actual event that created the stress and the memory of the event, which caused her to experience the exact same emotions of the original event.

Dispenza says "Therefore, the memory of an event can become branded neurologically in the brain, and that scene becomes frozen in time in our gray matter, just as it did for Anna. The combination of various people or objects at a particular time and place from that stressful experience is etched in our neural architecture as a holographic image. That's how we create a long-term memory. Therefore, the experience becomes imprinted in the neural circuitry, and the emotion is stored in the body—and that's how our past becomes our biology. In other words, when we experience a traumatic event, we tend to think neurologically within the circuitry of that experience and we tend to feel chemically within the boundaries of the emotions from the event, so our entire state of being— how we think and how we feel— becomes biologically stuck in the past."

Essentially, the painful thoughts we keep rehearsing continue to create suffering in us until it metastasizes. As it spreads, we also create susceptibility to more trauma and potentially infect those that love us with our pain. Depending on how we choose to move through our traumatic experiences, if we choose the path of pain, we can all be Anna on any given day.

Dr. Dispenza says it this way: "It's amazing how this can happen to so many people. Because of a shock or trauma in their lives, they never get beyond those corresponding emotions, and their health and their lives break down. If an addiction is something that you think you can't stop, then objectively it looks as though people like Anna become addicted to the very emotions of stress that are making them sick. The rush of adrenaline and the rest of the stress hormones arouse their brain and body, providing a rush of energy. In time, they become addicted to the rush of that chemistry—and then they use the people and conditions in their lives to reaffirm their addiction to the emotion, just to keep feeling that heightened state. Anna was using her stressful conditions to re-create that rush of energy, and without realizing it; she became emotionally addicted to a life she hated. Science tells us that such chronic, long-term stress pushes the genetic buttons that create disease. So if Anna was turning the stress response on by thinking about her problems and her past, her thoughts were making her sick. And since stress hormones are so powerful, she had become addicted to her own thoughts that were making her feel so bad..."

So how do we turn it around?

If our rehearsal of painful thoughts, old stories, and past traumatic experiences are the avenues we knowingly or unknowingly created to get to the Depression, then as beautiful, masterful creators we get to use the same magnitude of energy and momentum to recreate our path. As beautiful, masterful creators we get to recreate our story with new thoughts that fire up new neurons in our brain that will send new loving signals to our bodies, causing it to map out new genes and new healthy responses. We get to take the pen back and rewrite our story whenever we want to. Why? Because our minds are just that powerful.

We get to rewrite our story in a way that heals us and allows us to live from the love that we are, to live as the love we always have been and to live in the joy, peace, and freedom that is our birthright! We have to love ourselves better by first being aware of ourselves, being present with our thoughts, answering our own calls for love, and showing up for ourselves with the same vehement passion and commitment that we tend to use to show up for others. We have to commit to our own self-care. To think that you can let love and care come out of your being, bypass you, and be emitted to others is to be deluded and sadly mistaken. You can't effectively be something to someone that you haven't first been to yourself. So the best thing you can do for everyone else is to show up for you FIRST.

With the right self-care tools, some professional counseling and therapy, some deep breaths, self-love, self-compassion, self-patience, and regular rehearsing of positive thoughts for mind treatment, like Anna, you can become supernatural, move beyond your past and heal yourself. You are just that powerful.

With A Sound Mind,

Nadia

TODAY'S THOUGHT

"I keep my mind on things that create life. I keep my mind on things that make me come alive. When my mind is right, my life is right. I don't have to fight—just stay aligned"

— **PASTOR GREG STAMPER**

TODAY'S OVERCOMING DEPRESSION JOURNAL

Today, I found it challenging to overcome depression when

_____

_____

_____

_____

Today, I found it easy to overcome depression when

_____

_____

_____

_____

The key thought from Today's Chronicle I will focus on is

_____

_____

_____

_____

Self-Love Chronicle, No. 8

THE BEAUTY OF ISOLATION

TODAY'S CHRONICLE FROM NADIA

My Zen Friend,

The trees sway back and forth as a cool breeze comes through them and influences their dancing motion. It's a gentle breeze. I'm surrounded by so many that I can't count them. They obstruct my view, disabling me from seeing any other cabin around me. From their limbs emerge peach-inspired flowers whose center is blood red. Too far for me to reach out and smell them, I can only assume they have an exquisite aroma based on the queen-sized bees that can't seem to get enough of them. Like some game of hide and seek, I watch a bee rest on the lip of the flower and then disappear into its bulb, emerging moments later.

In the near distance, I hear a majestic song from a team of birds, complimented by the single chirps of another bird. It's the perfect harmony. The skies are sunny, bright, and clear. The air is crisp and still, only interrupted by the sound of a family in a nearby cabin. The sound is laughter! Very hearty laughter that permeates the trees in front of me, meeting my eardrum in the most pleasant way. It sounds like fun. It makes ME laugh. I can't see them, but I can HEAR them. I wish I knew what they were laughing at! Happiness is exactly what I hear alongside the sound of continuously moving water from the stream below. As I peer over the porch, I can't see where it begins. I wonder where it ends?

A hush comes over the air, my head is focused on the pen hitting my paper. Then out of nowhere, a bluebird swoops through the porch and startles me. I let out a deep sigh of relief as I grip my chest and pant. I'm instantly intrigued by its beauty. My eyes follow his every move. He wastes no time jumping on a few branches. Just as suddenly as he came, he vanishes!

Neither my anxiety nor my marvel lasted long. I'm alone, except for the company of my dog, Kyle, who's sitting on the wooden swing with me, surveying every sound he hears. I gently run my hands over his fluffy white fur. I'm not lonely. I'm accompanied by the solitude of my thoughts and the amazing grandeur of all God has created.   As I stopped, sat still, and listened, I could feel a calm peace settling in my inward parts that I've never known. I'm not frustrated, anxious, or worried about ANYTHING! I'm in the mountains, elevated above and isolated from the noise, the hustle, the bustle, and the demands of my everyday life.   Today, I could stop and appreciate the beauty of life in every form and I'm grateful! I'm grateful that peace interrupted my usual running thoughts and allowed me to look inward for answers and not outward. I stand in awe of the splendor of the Most High. This is the Awesomeness of God! Ahhhhhh! Isolation never felt so GOOD!

In Divine Glory,

Nadia

TODAY'S THOUGHT

I stand amazed at the splendor of your glory! Let every nation say just how GREAT you are! For you are holy... there is none like you; and you're perfect in everything you do! For you are Lord of ALL...The maker of Heaven and Earth! You are Lord of ALL...no one can compare to your worth. For you are holy! Holy are you Lord!!

— V. LAMAR WILSON, PSALMIST AND ARTIST

Today's BEAUTY OF ISOLATION Journal

Today, I found it challenging to embrace isolation when

_____

_____

_____

_____

Today, I found it easy to embrace isolation when

_____

_____

_____

_____

The key thought from Today's Chronicle I will focus on is

_____

_____

_____

_____

Self-Love Chronicle, No. 9

AUTHENTIC JOY

Often people attempt to live their lives backwards; they try to have more things, or more money, in order to do more of what they want, so they will be happier. The way it actually works is the reverse. You must first be who you really are, then do what you need to do, in order to have what you want.

—MARGARET YOUNG

Dear Sunshine,

It may be a challenge, but as much as you can, shift your thoughts and concerns from what others expect of you and live up to your own expectations of YOURSELF! Living up to your own expectations is so much more fulfilling than trying in vain to meet others' expectations. It's so cumbersome to focus on being who others think you should be. Create your own standard. Free yourself from the cares of anyone other than you and your God self. Feel the pressure being relieved, your true self being revealed, and your joy being unlocked. Sometimes it's as simple as changing your thought life in order that you may experience genuine joy. We hold OURSELVES captive to mental slavery and bonds. Change your mind! Shift from that old people-pleasing mentality. You're doing yourself and others a disservice by not being your truest self. You and you ONLY hold the key to your life's happiness; no one else is responsible for it!

You also aren't fooling anyone by buying all of the latest and greatest labels, brands, gadgets, houses, and cars while hanging out with "pretend friends" who only help you spend! When you're happy, both mentally and emotionally, with who you are, there isn't anything you can't have, do, or be because you'll be in tune with yourself enough to know just what you can and can't do. You won't live beyond your means. You won't try hard to impress others, and you won't live a lie and put on airs. It's stressful to keep putting on that mask. (Trust me, I've done it!) There's no joy in it AT ALL!! So "to thine own self be true."

Essentially, your joy isn't tied to material wealth or gain. Real joy is tied to loving and accepting who you are. In that moment where you breathe and get enough clarity to accept yourself as you are, so will other people. But it's your job to accept you FIRST. You can acquire all the "things" and acquaintances you want, but without real self-love, you'll still be unfulfilled. Get still. Remember to breathe. Be present. Discover YOU, learn YOU, be YOU, LOVE You, and the joy of life will follow!

With great joy,

TODAY'S THOUGHTS

Bliss is our highest purpose

—DEEPAK CHOPRA

When we connect to our true purpose in life, to whatever we've come to the planet to do, we get to live our lives in service and bliss...When we lay down the burden of trying to be anything other than exactly who we are, bliss comes to us effortlessly.

—OPRAH WINFREY

Joy is our highest purpose...Peace is our highest goal...and Love is our highest call

—NADIA (FACEBOOK POST, AUGUST 28, 2017)

TODAY'S AUTHENTIC JOY JOURNAL

Today, I found it challenging to authentically step into my joy

when_____

_____

_____

_____

Today, I found it easy to authentically step into my joy when

_____

_____

_____

_____

The key thought from Today's Chronicle I will focus on is

_____

_____

_____

_____

Part Two: The Value Chronicles

Value Chronicle, No. 1

PUTTING YOUR PRIDE ASIDE

TODAY'S CHRONICLE FROM NADIA

Hey My Love Bug,

NEWS FLASH: you no longer have to tap dance for handclaps! What is it that usually gets us puffed up, boasting, competing, haughty, and demonstrating downright arrogant behavior that is so opposite the Spirit of Love? Is it our never-ending need to impress others or meet their approval or standards? Is it our need or desperation for validation, constant recognition, or applause? Is it the well-performed tap dance we're doing to stay balanced on the pedestals we've been placed on? In most instances, we start out well. Our intentions are pure, our motives are sincere, and our posture is humble. When we begin a thing, we may be underexposed or inexperienced. The more exposure and experiences we have, the more we believe we know. The more we believe we know, the more confidence we build and the more others begin to tell us how "great" we are at what we do. If we allow it, these accolades, compliments, and constant "votes of confidence" start shaping our perception of how well we do in this area. It can feel validating if you aren't certain about who and whose you are. The compliments and ovations seemingly help us measure or gauge how "successful" we are. Once you feel like you've mastered "it," there isn't any one person who can compete with you in that area or knock you off of your pedestal! No one can tell you that you don't know your stuff--no one except the person who put you up on that pedestal.

You might ask, "Why would anybody want me to come down from a place that I've worked hard to get to?" This is your place of "greatness," right? WRONG! We have a very warped perception about what makes us great and it is usually associated with the way we are perceived by people. The Truth is you came here great. You never needed to work to prove that you are great. You just are.

The moment that our focus shifts from Love as our purely motivated cause to being motivated by applause, we are asking to be dethroned from our pompous, prideful, self-righteous pedestals to be realigned with the Truth. And the Universe will certainly respond. This is the destructive fall that haughtiness brings. The Spirit will never accept being second in command to the ego. Spirit knows no ego or anything that believes itself to be Spirit's opposite. Therefore, Spirit does not compete because in Truth there is no competitor. There is only Love.

Our driving force and motivation should always be about being a light, not about pleasing another flawed being or "thing" that we have allowed to take the place of our Highest Self. I often say, "Pride isn't the basis of our issues; the lack of clarity and certainty about our truest nature is where the problem begins." The moment we lay down our inherent greatness in exchange for people's validating and affirming opinions is the moment we can expect for The Universe to offer us a reality check. The noted theologian, Barnes, says this about the subject matter: "Whosoever exalteth himself will be humbled...This is universal among people, and it is also the way in which [The Universe] will deal with people. Men will perpetually endeavor to bring down those who endeavor to exalt themselves..." Theologian Matthew Henry adds: "Works of charity are better than works of show."

In the grander scheme, pride is derived from our bloodthirsty, insatiable ego. It's no secret that the ego never serves us well because it is counterproductive to our inherent state of being love and light in the world. So as much as you can and as often as you can, disidentify with the ego and all of its limitations; it is rooted in fear. It's not loving nor will it ever be. Lead from love, not pride. Walk in the light of...

Humbly,

Nadia

TODAY'S THOUGHT

*Work for a cause, not for applause.
You're only as great as the people
you have served!*

TODAY'S PRIDE JOURNAL

Today, I found it challenging to release my pride when

_____

_____

_____

_____

Today, I found it easy to release my pride when

_____

_____

_____

_____

The key thought from Today's Chronicle I will focus on is

_____

_____

_____

_____

Value Chronicle, No. 2

THE STING OF REJECTION

Hey My Sweets!

I used to be quite the people pleaser. Now, c'mon! Don't read this in such disbelief. Who, Nadia? Yes, Nadia! I think we have all desired to be validated by the people that matter to us. If we were to be completely honest, we've even sought approval from people who DON'T really matter, but had an opinion about us in some way that we valued. My problem was accepting that I wasn't like everybody else, never would be, and didn't need to be. I've ALWAYS been different, unique, not the norm, not average, and not status quo...a "free spirit", if you will. As you can imagine I never really have "fit in." I became all too familiar with seeming rejection of all sorts very early on in life. I've been told a lot of what I'm "too much of" such as,

You're too flirtatious.

You're too short.

You're too friendly.

Your hair is too wild.

Your clothes are too much.

You sing too loud.

You act too silly.

You're too talkative.

You're too serious.

You're too tomboyish.

You work too hard.

You're too dramatic.

You have too many tattoos.

You're too business-minded.

You're too spiritual!

I'm too NADIA, I suppose!? Not even possible. I am enough just as I am.

Can I tell you that more than half of these critiques came from close friends, family, and co-laborers? These are the very people I looked to for approval and validation, not personal scrutiny and discouragement. If you digest them, these heavy opinions can do quite a number on your self-esteem, leaving you in fear that you'll never be good enough, never measure up, never get "it" quite right, and never be enough of the right "stuff"! If I choose to spend my life listening to all of the people who are "too" opinionated about how much of "me" they prefer, I'd be left to be NOTHING. But I choose the Truth that I'm more than enough. Pastor Yolanda Batts says it this way, "God doesn't create from a place of "too much." It creates from ever-expanding good. There is no such thing as "too much."

I have learned to be [mindful] about the voices I allow to be validating in my life. Some of the most critical people I've encountered couldn't carry my cross or bear my lot for a full sixty seconds. The reality is, you're absolutely entitled to your opinion but I'm also entitled to consider the source! While I am an advocate for personal growth and introspection, I am also increasingly aware of the fact that people who are not grounded in their own self-love, self-awareness, self-worth, and self-confidence are never going to be satisfied no matter how many personality adjustments you make! [They can only see you through the lenses of their own feelings of inadequacy, limitations, and fear.

And you know what else? You can't make EVERYBODY happy and their happiness is none of your business. Your business is YOUR happiness so shift your focus to governing your own happiness. You're somebody's cup of tea! You won't have your personality rearranged and edited by EVERY person you meet. I have reached a place where after much sorting and sifting through seeming rejection, I like me and I'm FINALLY comfortable in the skin I'm in! The moment I stopped trying to be someone other than myself, I realized that what I really am is "too" focused on my purpose, "too" driven, "too" perfectly imperfect, and "too" great within my own right to be stifled by the opinions of others. And I'm grateful for those experiences that guided me to this awareness.

Sometimes who you are and all you come with is intimidating to those who may not be in tune with their own greatness.

Sometimes people recognize your greatness before you embrace or acknowledge it in yourself. They always knew you'd be great, and now they see how much you are coming into the awareness of the greatness they saw all along. Sometimes your uniqueness or peculiarity makes them uncomfortable in their average skin! People will criticize whatever they don't understand.

We often criticize others based on the depth of our understanding. Our understanding is shaped by our knowledge. Our knowledge is rooted in our limited experiences and information. Our limited perceptions are often the premise on which we stand to proclaim, "I disagree," "I don't like that," "That's a shame," "Why would he do that?," "That don't make no sense," or "See, if it was me, I woulda..." We make our flawed selves the standard ALL. THE. TIME.

Instead of asking questions, studying, or researching, we turn to being critical about something we know little about because it's easier than doing what it takes to get an understanding. Just because you don't know about something doesn't make it wrong, it just makes you ignorant. The best cure for ignorance is information. Educate yourself before you judge others. If you don't want to be informed, just be quiet. But certainly don't reject others on the basis of what you would or wouldn't do or who you believe yourself to be. Live and let live.

No matter the test, the trial, or the magnitude of rejection we experience, we don't HAVE to lie there and accept it. We can be empowered by rejection and go on to GREATNESS. Just in case no one's ever told you, let me be the first: it's OK to be your authentic self. You are WORTHY—and you are MORE THAN ENOUGH!

In my own skin,

Nadia

TODAY'S THOUGHT

No one knows your path to greatness better than you, so expect that the very lack of understanding will cause some rejection. People will often criticize and reject what they don't understand.

TODAY'S RELEASING REJECTION JOURNAL

Today, I found it challenging to release rejection when

_____

_____

_____

_____

Today, I found it easy to release rejection when

_____

_____

_____

_____

The key thought from Today's Chronicle I will focus on is

_____

_____

_____

_____

Value Chronicle, No. 3

THE POWER OF SILENCE

Dear Powerful One,

Yⁿou cannot afford to not be aware of your power. But what does it mean to BE powerful? Merriam Webster defines power as follows:

1. The ability or capacity to perform or act effectively.

2. A specific capacity, faculty, or aptitude. Often used in the plural: her powers of concentration.

3. Strength or force exerted or capable of being exerted; might; strength.

4. The ability or official capacity to exercise control; authority.

Sometimes we willingly yet unknowingly hand our power over to people. We do so when we aren't aware of what we say, how we say it, and when we speak out in anger, jealousy, frustration, and insecurity. Speaking without power indicates a lack of self-control and authority. Essentially, speaking rashly is indicative of a lack of power. We have a tendency to attend every argument we're invited to, and when we lose control, we plant corrupt seeds and create corrupt worlds with our words. We call forth things that are not as though they were through the power of our words!

There's a proverb that I love that says, "The tongue has the power of life and death, and those who love it will eat its fruit."

(Proverbs 18:21) We can always choose the fruit we'll eat. There is sometimes more power in SILENCE than there are in words. Learn to BE QUIET! If you silence your mouth, you can deny people access to your other portals of power, which are your mind and your heart.

With silent authority,

Nadia

TODAY'S THOUGHT

Silence is more than golden; it is a POWER all its own! Being mindful of what you say is a precaution in giving away your power!

Shhhhhh!

TODAY'S POWER OF SILENCE JOURNAL

Today, I found it challenging to embrace the power of silence

when_____

_____

_____

_____

Today, I found it easy to embrace the power of silence when

_____

_____

_____

_____

The key thought from Today's Chronicle I will focus on is

_____

_____

_____

_____

Value Chronicle, No. 4

THE APPETITE OF GREED

Dear Friend,

When we consider greed, we mostly associate it with food or the unending desire for more money. Naturally, those are the surface results of greed but not necessarily the root cause. Have you ever considered that what keeps you with an unsatisfied appetite is your lack of gratitude? Do you treat your inexpensive clothes like you do your labels? Probably not. Do you make sure your Ford Taurus is as well kept as your Mercedes Benz? Not likely. Why is that? Because we have a strong affinity for excess and trends. Before we can enjoy the one we have, we have already gotten another one to replace it. You tell yourself, "Everybody has one and surely I have to keep up!" We hardly give ourselves a chance to appreciate anything, and, therefore, we don't value what we have. If we don't value it, there is no way we can be grateful for it.

Don't believe it? Give your excess clothes, shoes, and such to a person who doesn't have the means to readily purchase things the way that you can. Feed a full meal to a person who normally scavenges the dumpsters for food. Provide even an air mattress for a person who normally sleeps on a sidewalk or park bench. Give toiletries to a homeless woman who normally has to sort out how she will deal with menstruation every month while living on the streets. Show love and affection to a person who's hardly ever experienced it. You will see a picture of gratitude that can't be compared! They know what it is to not have. Now, that they have, they value it, appreciate it, and that lends itself to being grateful!

If we take on the attitude of the missionary that the Bible documents as Paul instead of one of never being satisfied, we'll be more susceptible to gratitude. In Philippians 4:11-12 New Living Translation (NLT) Paul says, "I am not saying this because I am in need, for I have learned to be content whatever the circumstances. I know what it is to be in need, and I know what it is to have plenty. I have learned the secret of being content in any and every situation, whether well fed or hungry, whether living in plenty or in want.

I often say and believe that "gratitude breeds abundance." Then it stands to reason that complaining begets lack. The remedy for greed or feelings of not having enough is not overindulging and accumulating things. If you want more, look around you, take note of all that you DO have, be grateful for all of the abundance that is surrounding you, and give thanks for it all. When you do that, you'll realize the abundance you've been longing for is the abundance you've been living with all along.

Modestly,

Nadia

TODAY'S THOUGHT

The reason you want every single thing that you want is because you think you will feel really good when you get there. But if you don't feel really good when on your way to there, you can't get there. You have to be satisfied with what is while you're reaching for more.

— ABRAHAM-HICKS

TODAY'S RELEASING GREED JOURNAL

Today, I found it challenging to release greed when

_____

_____

_____

_____

Today, I found it easy to release greed when

_____

_____

_____

_____

The key thought from Today's Chronicle I will focus on is

_____

_____

_____

_____

Value Chronicle, No. 5

THE FEAR OF FEAR

Hey Faith Walker!

In the 2005 critically acclaimed movie Coach Carter, Samuel L. Jackson plays a coach who challenges his misfit basketball underdogs. He pushes them harder than they had ever been pushed because he saw the greatness in them. Despite the fact that most of these students came from impoverished backgrounds and meager upbringings and never saw their parents, peers, or anyone from their neighborhoods do much with their own lives, Coach Carter knew he could help to dispel the myth that they would be a product of their environment. He knew he could change their lives if they could see their own potential.

Coach Carter keeps asking his players, "What's your deepest fear?" and for quite a while the players don't understand the question or why it was asked. Finally, one of the players, Timo Cruz, responds with the following quote by author Marianne Williamson:

Our deepest fear is not that we are inadequate. Our deepest fear is that we are powerful beyond measure. It is our light, not our darkness, that most frightens us. Your   p l a y i n g small does not serve the world. There is nothing enlightened about shrinking so that other people won't feel insecure around you. We are all meant to shine as children do. It's not just in some of us; it is in everyone. And as we let our own lights shine, we unconsciously give other people permission to do the same. As we are liberated from our own fear, our presence automatically liberates others.

Sometimes the fear we carry does not originate with us. We often adopt the fears of others. We especially inherit their fears when that is all we have seen in those who shape or lead us. We rehearse the thought that their story is our story. We believe that since "it" happened to them, "it" will inevitably happen to us. We go on to fear being greater and better than who or what we have come from. We fear that others will think we have "forgotten where we've come from" and be in a better position than them. We fear being our best because we have convinced ourselves that we may not be able to maintain that level of greatness. We fear disappointing others. Every time we're given an opportunity to be better than we are, we do something to sabotage it because we fear being as GREAT as we know we can be. We prefer to believe the lies that fear tell us versus the truth that helps us to believe. Our fears are rooted in lies and illusions that appear to be real. The Truth is fear has no origin. It has no Source, no Creator, or no parents, so to speak. Just like darkness has no switch and is merely the absence of light, fear is the absence of love.

My former band director, Willie E. Lyles, would say, "Perfect practice makes PERFECT!" I urge you to practice exercising, employing, and constantly using your faith and it will become your habit. The more you practice, faith will become your

INSTANT reaction to fear. Your habit of faith will then become your lifestyle.

In Faith,

Nadia

TODAY'S THOUGHT

Never fear what you don't know because fear will certainly make sure you NEVER find out!

TODAY'S RELEASING FEAR JOURNAL

Today, I found it challenging to release fear when

_____

_____

_____

_____

Today, I found it easy to release fear when

_____

_____

_____

_____

The key thought from Today's Chronicle I will focus on is

_____

_____

_____

_____

Value Chronicle, No. 6

WHEN YOUR FAITH NEEDS FAITH

God grant me the serenity to accept the things I cannot change; Courage to change the things I can; and the wisdom to know the difference.

Dear Faithful One,

I have prayed this prayer more times than I can count. I usually find myself in this concentrated recitation at the point where my faith has started to wane. It happens right when what I have envisioned and what I actually see are severely incongruent. Therein lies the problem. I'm expecting to see the unseen from a physical, seeing world when what I'm hoping and believing for is still in the unseen realm. The only thing that even allows a thought to come to fruition is the power of believing unwaveringly that it CAN and WILL happen. I have to "faith" it into being! But usually what happens (besides the usual impatience we experience!) is we start trying to manufacture our own blessings by crafting a clone of what we envisioned. We create this clone instead of believing in a thing until we see it manifest just the way Spirit showed it to us. That manufacturing is an indication that doubt and disbelief are present. As an act of faith, we should certainly walk towards the thing we are envisioning, as this will indicate to God that our faith is fully activated. Our faith will cause us to move forward, not come to a complete standstill. But it should never cause us to start bootlegging God's best for us.

Case and point: You're single. You're not only believing God for a mate, but it's been spoken over your life on several occasions. You have had visions of your life with this person. In faith, you begin preparing yourself for marriage. You plan the wedding. You take cooking or baking classes. You read books on parenting and how to be a good mate. You play love songs and dance around your house. These are some of the works that will keep your faith alive as you wait with knowingness. If you truly believe in God for your future partner, it wouldn't make sense to just make your mate. You wouldn't just give credence, space, energy, and instruction to every Joe Blow that appears to have potential. You will wait for the Divine right partner you've prayed for.

Faith is the only thing we have that connects us in this seeing world to an unseen, ever-present God. The essence of faith is believing indubitably in what we hope for but have never seen beyond our vision or dream. Sometimes in our humanness we will become doubtful because we are influenced by mostly what we see. In those instances, our faith needs a little more faith!

With sincerity,

TODAY'S THOUGHT

*Recharge your faith
with a little more faith.*

TODAY'S INCREASING YOUR FAITH JOURNAL

Today, I found it challenging to increase my faith when

_____

_____

_____

_____

Today, I found it easy to increase my faith when

_____

_____

_____

_____

The key thought from Today's Chronicle I will focus on is

_____

_____

_____

_____

Value Chronicle, No. 7

NO JUDGMENT REQUIRED

Dear You,

If God be for me, who can be against me? Who can oppose me? Whom should I fear? What can man do to me? Who can bring any charges, allegations, or judgments against me as God's good idea? If God still loves me and deems me worthy, knowing all there is to know about me, who are you to decide that I'm unlovable, spiritually ineffective, or not anointed? Are you saying you are without flaws or imperfections? Have you made yourself "the standard"?

This is a small a sketch of what it looks like when we measure others with ourselves. We juxtapose others with ourselves as though we are the standard of righteousness. Then we decide, based on who we are or what we would do, that others are not as worthy, holy, righteous, saved, anointed, gifted, or as spiritual as we are. This man-made measuring system is usually based on some exterior attribute or behavior. Ironically, that system is completely opposite the one Source uses—Love.

Don't try living up to man-made, impossible standards that not even God expects. When faced with the judgment of other humans (even your pastor or religious leader!), just ask yourself, "If God is for me, then who can be against me?" (inspired by Romans 8:31). The truth is God knows us and has always known us as his own. The way God's Love is set up, nothing we can do can separate us from this unconditional love. His judgment system is one of everlasting, unending, unfailing love! And Source will never change Its mind about us. It sees us just the way it created us—perfect, whole, and complete and Its good idea.

Even when you find YOURSELF judging others, remind yourself of the following: I must operate within the confines of my own grace. Everyone's "thorns" are different and so is their grace. Study the art of silence and learn how to attend to your own affairs. It will give you the time you need to tremble at the thought of how much fine-tuning and improvement your soul's salvation needs.

There is NEVER any judgment required. The massive sea of unlovely things that you are constantly recalling and replaying in your mind, God isn't keeping a record! They are forever gone into the sea of forgetfulness. Though your issues, hang-ups, and mishaps seem to be somewhere in the "offender's abyss", someone may throw out their line to fish it out of your past. That "someone" is likely you. Let yourself off of the hook; when you do, it will be that much easier to extend grace to others. Be mindful the stones you hurl. None of us are exempt from life's lessons. We are all doing the best we can with what we know. We should all be in anticipation for the dawning of a new day (new thoughts, ideas, awakenings, enlightenments) when our mercy will be renewed. The good news is Love can cover what condemnation can't.

Mercifully,

TODAY'S THOUGHT

Judge and you will be judged. Be merciful and you will be shown mercy in proportionate measures.

TODAY'S JUDGMENT-FREE JOURNAL

Today, I found it challenging to free myself from judgment

when_____

_____

_____

_____

Today, I found it easy to free myself from judgment when

_____

_____

_____

_____

The key thought from Today's Chronicle I will focus on is

_____

_____

_____

_____

Value Chronicle, No. 8

WHO SAYS YOU FAILED?

TODAY'S CHRONICLE FROM NADIA

Dear Free Being,

Too often, we take on others' definition of something and make it our traditional view or perspective. If no one has ever told you that it's okay to think outside of the box and define your own standards, today I'm giving you permission to think for yourself.

Let's consider the word "failure." According to most dictionary definitions failure is the state or condition of not meeting a desirable or intended objective. Failure may also be viewed as the opposite of success. Failure is also determined by how you define success (remember we talked about success in Part One: The Self-Love Chronicles?).

There are times in my life when I considered myself unsuccessful at something, while others may have thought what I did was a major success. How did we both witness the same thing and come out with two different views? Easily. They viewed my "accomplishment" as a success because I completed the goals or requirements set before me for that particular task. However, I viewed it as a failure because I did not attain MY personal goals. Others were ecstatic and more than satisfied. Me, on the other hand? I was disappointed in myself and I wanted another opportunity to prove to myself that I could do better.

Your standard for success is inextricably tied to your perspective on failure and what you energize as truth. It is even safe to say that one man's success is another man's failure, and one man's failure is another man's success. Only you can determine what failure is for you. Take your job, for example. In a hypothetical scenario, your supervisor has a standard and you have your own personal goals. At your last review, he gave you a modified performance plan because you didn't hit your numbers last quarter. As you assessed what kept you from meeting his standards, you realized your issue was time management. You made the necessary adjustments to improve in that area. While you did not meet EVERY expectation set forth in the modified performance plan, you achieved your personal goal of mastering the skill of time management. Mastering that skill helped to significantly improve your job performance.

So you didn't get the numbers your supervisor wanted— did you FAIL? Absolutely not! Improvement can never be considered a failure! If improvement was your goal, and you achieved it, it is then a complete success. You'll have more opportunities to "meet the numbers" provided that you keep improving.

Let me offer you another perspective. From where I'm standing, the only way to fail is to give up before you try, talk yourself out of success, self-sabotage your opportunity, or energize the very thing you don't want with fear. If you underestimate your ability to improve and convince yourself that at every attempt the outcome will be the same as when things didn't go well, then you have willingly chosen not to believe the best about yourself on your path to greatness. You have emitted a vibration of "throwing in the towel" and, essentially, you created an adverse outcome that is counterproductive to the Spirit's predetermined victory for you. The Universe will simply respond, "Yes" to whatever vibration you put out.

For example, you might think, "Oh I'm no good at this anyway. I don't even know why I tried. It's not even my thing. Other people are far better at this. There's no sense in me doing this. It would just never work out."

And The Universe simply replies with, "OK! Sure thing! Yes! And so it is!"

See how that works? The Universe is not here to filter through what you REALLY mean versus what you energized as your truth during a point of real, charged up momentum. As the old adage cautions: "Be careful what you wish for, it might just come true."

Now you might be questioning, "Nadia, how do I get to the victoriously fixed outcome that is planned for me? Well, I thought you'd never ask! It will require you to shift your consciousness to the truth about who and whose you are. A Course In Miracles says it this way: "If you knew who walks beside you on the way that you have chosen, fear would be impossible." The truth is that you and God are one. If there is no failure in God, then there is also no failure in YOU! God is Love, and there is no fear in Love. Love and fear can't co-exist.

So as Abraham-Hicks alludes to, God will not follow you down the path of your fear. Love will not join you for a sit-down dinner at the feast of fear. Fear is only an illusion. It's that thing that happens when you have forgotten that you are Love. The moment that you remember who you are, whose you are, and who walks beside you on your path, you return to the victory that Love predestined for you. There is no failure in Love; therefore, there is no failure in you. There are only lessons and opportunities to keep showing up for yourself so you can be better and better all the time.

Fearlessly Successful,

Nadia

TODAY'S THOUGHTS

Show me where I have second chances and I'll show you that I've never failed! If there's always room for improvement, then there are always opportunities for success. I will never quit, thus I will never fail. I Am Love and Love walks beside me.

I CAN'T fear and I CAN'T fail!

TODAY'S LEARNING FROM FAILURE JOURNAL

Today, I found it challenging to see my failure as a learning

opportunity when_____

_____

_____

_____

Today, I found it easy to see my failure as a learning opportunity

when_____

_____

_____

_____

The key thought from Today's Chronicle I will focus on is

_____

_____

_____

_____

Value
Chronicle, No. 9

HOW TO LOSE LIKE A CHAMP

TODAY'S CHRONICLE FROM NADIA

Dear Victorious One,

I vividly recall my first competitive loss. I was in the fifth grade. I was a spelling bee champ much like Keke Palmer's character in Akeelah and the Bee. I had a knack for vocabulary and I was a force to be reckoned with. But I was only aware of MY "force" and not the other spelling bee "forces." As far as I understood and experienced, I couldn't be beat. At the final round, only me and Larry Cochran (who I had defeated before) were left standing. I was so focused on me that I didn't consider his "force," and I lost to him that day. Larry had an advantage over me--he had lost before. His loss became his driving force. Larry had a power I knew nothing about. He was DETERMINED to win, while I, on the other hand, took winning for granted. He deserved to win. I needed to lose that day. I needed an opportunity to acquire that very same power, drive, and hunger!

Over the course of my nearly 40 years, I have experienced more loss than I care to recount. But I now notice a pattern in my losing: I ALWAYS emerge stronger, better, and more determined—just like Larry was. Most people get so discouraged, intimidated, and paralyzed by loss that they spiral into eternal defeat. Loss is not intended to show you how powerless you are. It is there to help you recognize how to strengthen your next win! Just because I lost that one spelling bee, it didn't mean I was a complete failure. It reminded me to never get comfortable with being average. While Larry strategized, studied longer and harder, and fueled himself with the power of his previous defeat, I coasted, rested on my laurels, and I got a rude awakening. But it was an awakening nonetheless!   Although I lost to Larry, both he and I had qualified to represent our school on a district-wide level. I had no time to sulk and wallow in the sting of defeat. I had to regroup, refocus, re-strategize, and come back with a vengeance.

What I learned is that loss keeps me on my toes. If I had never lost, I could never appreciate winning. Loss is NECESSARY. In the grand scheme of things, the only thing I lost was my pride. My pride was something that I needed to lose in order to win to a greater magnitude. I realize that if I compete and I'm not chosen, in the end I won't lose if I put my pride aside, and give it my very best shot.

Make the determination to be empowered by your loss, and lose like a champ. All the greats before us have done it and have much to show for it. Why would I be any different? You only really lose when you stop trying and allow defeat to stifle you. We are not defined by our wins or losses. We are defined by how we respond to winning or losing. The attitude of a champion is not, "Oh well, I lost! I'll never do that again. I'm a horrible failure!" A champion's attitude says "Better luck next time. Let me start preparing for the next opportunity NOW! I need to be ready for the force I will meet!"

I've learned to appreciate every loss because it has made me a better WINNER!! My attitude is everything, so even when I lose, I win! As Nelson Mandela put it, "I never lose; I either win or learn."

With a champion's heart,

Nadia

TODAY'S THOUGHTS

Winning is not a sometime thing; it's an all time thing. You don't win once in a while, you don't do things right once in a while, you do them right all the time. Winning is habit. Unfortunately, so is losing.

— VINCE LOMBARDI

The greatest test of courage on earth is to bear defeat without losing heart

—ROBERT GREEN INGERSOLL

Lose well! Win BETTER!

—NADIA R. PERRY

TODAY'S LOSING LIKE A CHAMPION JOURNAL

Today, I found it challenging to accept and learn from my

losses when_____

_____

_____

_____

Today, I found it easy to accept and learn from my losses when

_____

_____

_____

_____

The key thought from Today's Chronicle I will focus on is

_____

_____

_____

_____

Part Three:
The Purpose
Chronicles

Purpose Chronicle, No. 1

WRITE YOUR VISION, MAKE IT PLAIN

Dear Beautiful Being,

Some might argue that when a vision is given to you, you should just remember the way it was shown and begin living it out. If this is the philosophy you have used for carrying out your vision, there is no wondering about why it may not have panned out. I've seen many formulas for "success" and I've heard many people give testament to how their vision came to fruition. I even like the latest trend of doing a vision board. Depending on where you are on your path, it's a great tool to jumpstart your manifesting mind. Personally, Dr. Michael Beckwith's Visioning process has been one of the most beneficial tools in my manifestor's tool bag. These methodologies most closely align themselves with the instructions Spirit gave to the prophet Habakkuk as documented in the Bible.   As the story goes, Habakkuk is perplexed by the enormous amount of evil in the land of Judah and is having a dialogue with God about it because he feels God should be doing more than what he sees God doing. Sound familiar? Habakkuk still wrestles with God. Habakkuk now riddled with impatience, has more questions for God and gets the following answer:

Then the Lord answered me and said: Write the vision And make it plain on tablets, That he may run who reads it. For the vision is yet for an appointed time; But at the end it will speak, and it will not lie. Though it tarries, wait for it; Because it will   surely come, It will not tarry. (Habakkuk 2: 2-3)

As I studied this passage, I extracted the following four things you need to do in order to get your vision jumpstarted and see the fruit of your labor:

1. Write down your vision. Regardless of whether you use a vision board, a "I Am" board, record your goals using audio or video, or create your vision with someone else, develop a practical way for you to see and begin realizing your vision of and for yourself every day.

2. Make your vision easily understandable. If someone must take the torch and run with it, write your vision so clearly that it can be carried out.

3. Execute your vision with the right timing. Seek God's divine guidance on the right time to begin bringing your vision to life.

4. No matter how long it takes, wait for your vision to come to fruition. Don't give up midway on the journey. Whatever you envision, it WILL come to be! Amen, Ase', and so it is!

Patiently awaiting manifestation,

Nadia

TODAY'S THOUGHT

Write the vision! Make it plain!

TODAY'S CREATING YOUR VISION JOURNAL

Today, I found it challenging to step into and create my vision

when_____

_____

_____

_____

Today, I found it easy to step into and create my vision when

_____

_____

_____

_____

The key thought from Today's Chronicle I will focus on is

_____

_____

_____

_____

Purpose Chronicle, No. 2

ENDURING PAIN WITH A PURPOSE

If there's no breaking then there's no healing, and if there's no healing then there's no learning.

— ONE TREE HILL

Hey My Sweetheart,

Let's face it--we can't go our entire lives with absolutely NO pain! It's unrealistic to believe that it's even possible! Regardless of whether it is self-inflicted or imposed on you by someone else, the hurts, pains, heartaches, disappointments, and seeming brokenness all have a purpose. One of the greatest purposes is to awaken to our lack of awareness and to be reminded to be present. Iyanla Vanzant created the following beautiful acronym for the word P.A.I.N.—Pay Attention Inward Now. We need to acknowledge that we have in some way or another attracted this experience into our lives. Once this experience arrives into our energetic space, it is accompanied by a life lesson. With every lesson brought by our most challenging moments comes an opportunity to also teach others.   In the lowest moments of my healing processes, one of the driving forces that kept me moving forward were the people that I knew I would be able to help if I could just move through the difficulty with grace and gratitude instead of resistance. I knew that once I healed, it would give so many others permission to heal. American artist Yoko Ono put it this way: "Healing yourself is connected with healing others." It's so much bigger than you!

Sometimes people need to see an example, hear a testimony, have some form of proof that it is possible to overcome, and know that it's OK to end the pain. Every time a person chooses to end their pain, they unconsciously invite in lessons and growth. They invite their awareness to be awakened and recognize patterns, cycles, behaviors, pathologies, and generational imprinting. They invite the eyes of their enlightenment to be opened to be a student first, then a teacher. They invite wholeness, peace, liberty, and love into their innermost being. They invite an opportunity to let go of their attachments to anything and anyone that is no longer serving them well. They invite their healing!

Ever healing, ever growing,

Nadia

TODAY'S THOUGHTS

*All of life is a movement towards
our wholeness*

—PASTOR GREG STAMPER

*Some pain is necessary and all
pain has a purpose!*

TODAY'S PURPOSE-DRIVEN JOURNAL

Today, I found it challenging to be on purpose when

_____

_____

_____

_____

Today, I found it easy to be on purpose when

_____

_____

_____

_____

The key thought from Today's Chronicle I will focus on is

_____

_____

_____

_____

Purpose Chronicle, No. 3

THE GOOD FRUIT OF PATIENCE

Dear Patient One,

If you saw my mom and I separately, you probably wouldn't think we looked alike. She has beautiful chocolate skin, while she considers me more pecan tan or caramel. She has full lips, a broad nose, a hereditary gap in her teeth, a 5'5" size 12/14 frame, and sexy bowlegs. Me? I'm 4'11", size 3 frame, slender, athletic build, broad forehead, the hereditary teeth gap and, according to my mom, I have a "flat pappy nose and a crooked grin" like my father. If you've never seen my dad, then when I'm standing next to my mom you'll see enough of a resemblance to tell we're related. But ask anyone who knew or has seen my dad and they'd tell you I'm his spitting image; my mom agrees. She'd tell anybody who declared that she and I look alike: "Really? I don't think so; she looks JUST like her dad so much until it's eerie." Although my mom and I don't look alike, you can tell that I'm her child. I sing like my dad, but I SOUND like my mom. The phone rings at her house. I answer "Hello...?" Caller: "Hey Dean..." And then the caller proceeds to converse with me as if I'm my mom. I chuckle and say, "This is Nadia, lemme get mama for ya". My mom is rather reserved and a bit of an introvert, but when she gets dressed boy, oh boy does she turn on the confidence! It's usually a conversation piece because she had what her former co-workers called "a million dollar walk." But the bigger conversation in our family is how LONG it takes her to get dressed—or to do anything, for that matter! She is admittedly "slow as a turtle," which is a trait

I apparently inherited. Let my friends tell it, I'm the slowest person they have EVER met! I go, "REALLY? But I'm faster than anyone in my family!" We all inherited my mom's careful, meticulous but slow nature. Now talk about a lady who can cook and bake?! Hands down, my mama is THEE BEST! And guess what? Me and my siblings inherited her cooking skills, although only my sister and I having baking skills just like my mom. My mom is one of the most resilient, kind, loving, and forgiving souls I know. When others take note of those same qualities in me, I am aware that those traits were imprinted on me by my mom.

Regardless of whether or not my mom and I physically resemble each other, there is NO DOUBT that I'm her child because I have her fruit!   We all recognize an apple tree when we see one, right? How? Because of the fruit it bears! When you are of God, you can't fool anyone; your fruit (or the lack thereof) will let people know! Patience is a fruit or attribute of God and we know that because of how extremely patient Spirit is with us. You can't be in, of, or love God and have short patience, a short fuse, or a quick temper.

It's no easy feat to be patient, particularly when you live in a "have it your way, right away" society. But in the grander scheme of things, who wants ANYTHING that is under-ripe, ill-fitting, unsuitable, unready, improperly prepared, poorly manufactured or constructed, and just plain ole undone? Sure it took the mechanic more time than you would have liked to repair your car, but now it "purrs like a kitten." Sure it took your husband a year to finish having the kitchen remodeled, but now you have exactly what you wanted. Of course, dinner wasn't done when you came in, but your wife took her time to put her heart and soul into it so it'd be just what the doctor ordered when it hit your belly. So what you didn't get the promotion on the first, second or third try? TRY AGAIN and wait until it's your turn so you'll get the promotion designed just for you! That business venture didn't "jump off" as quickly as you would have liked, so you got weary. Jump back in there; you dreamed it, you birthed it out...now you have to raise it patiently while it fully manifests. Be patient with yourself and then you'll be patient with others.

One of the most powerful evidences of love is PATIENCE. The first being who should experience this from you is YOU! Be patient with yourself. Stay away from self-sabotage, martyrdom, perfectionism and self-criticism. If that's the way you treat yourself, then unquestionably that's how you'll treat others. If you're more patient with yourself then quite naturally you'll be more patient towards others. Stop and look introspectively, breathe, and then ask yourself, "Am I being too hard on myself? Am I inflicting that same behavior on everyone around me?"

If you said "yes" to the first question then it's highly likely that you'll have to give a "yes" to the second question. As a matter of fact, you can put any attribute or description in that space and search yourself: "Do I doubt myself? Do I trust myself? Am I honest with myself?" How you answer those internal questions is likely a reflection of how you interact with others. You're with yourself more than anyone else, is, so take the time to KNOW yourself, be TRUE to yourself, and LOVE yourself! And when you are your best self for YOU, you can't help but be your best self to and for others.

Just remember that as you embark on the never-ending journey to self-love, you will discover things about you that you didn't know were there and these things may not always be very flattering, but they are true nonetheless! That is the very place where you will need to show yourself the best love you can by being patient with yourself! We are all reflections of each other; every person we encounter is a mirror of who we are in some way. If you don't like the reflection, work on the image, not the mirror! If you find that others are impatient with you...well, I think you know where this is going! Maybe you are impatient with yourself and others that you think you're loving so well! Love is Patient! Love yourself!

Loving you infinitely,

TODAY'S THOUGHT

Anything worth having is worth waiting for patiently! Don't just check your brother or sister—Check YOUR fruit! Love Yourself!

TODAY'S PATIENCE JOURNAL

Today, I found it challenging to practice patience when

_____

_____

_____

_____

Today, I found it easy to practice patience when

_____

_____

_____

_____

The key thought from Today's Chronicle I will focus on is

_____

_____

_____

_____

Purpose Chronicle, No. 4

INTIMACY: YOU DON'T REALLY KNOW ME!

"Who? Her? Oh yeah! I know her!"

"Who? Ole boy's brother?
Yeah I know dat dude."

TODAY'S CHRONICLE FROM NADIA

Dear "Friend,"

D on't you just hate when people claim they "know" you even though they've only met you once or twice? Or how about the people who have stalked your social media so much until they think they have you ALL figured out? Or the folks who know your relatives and casually met you in passing but feel well versed enough on you to give someone a character description of you? Then there are the people who grew up with you and haven't seen you since elementary school and they tell people how well they know you as if you're still in Mrs. Brown's third-grade class. The same happens with former or current co-workers you never see beyond the cubicle; choir and church members you never engage beyond the vestibule; and mere acquaintances you shared a few hi-and-bye exchanges with. After a few brief encounters, people seem to think they REALLY know you! Don't you just despise that? I even have family members who don't KNOW me! It just goes to show you how wrongly people interpret what it is to "know" somebody.

I have a few different circles of friends but each of them are very intimate circles. We spend quality time with each other getting up close and personal, sharing sacred information and experiences, and revealing parts of our innermost beings that no outside person would be privy to. I can tell them the things about me that aren't so flattering without fear of judgment or ridicule. I bare it all to them with the confidence that they will tell me the truth about myself (and vice versa) in the most loving, respectful way possible. I never fear letting my guard down and being candid with them, neither do I worry that they will expose me or tell my personal information to anyone else. This tried-and-true bond allows me to be comfortable to reveal to them more about myself with time. I can talk to them about my fears, insecurities, shortcomings, hurts, struggles AND I can share my visions, goals, dreams, ambitions, and successes. THAT is intimacy!

Intimacy is not so much about a touch, a kiss, a snuggle, a caress, or getting physically disrobed. As I have learned from Apostle Ron Carpenter (one of the spiritual leaders I highly respect), intimacy is information. The closer you get to someone, the more personal you all become. The more personal you become, the more trusting and comfortable you are with them. The more trusting and comfortable you can be, the more information you share. The more information you share, the more they KNOW you at the heart of who you really are. Only those closest and most intimate with me REALLY know me. They get to experience me in each moment as I unfold, sift, sort, evolve, and navigate my path. Intimacy allows them to grow with me and learn me as I'm constantly learning myself. THAT is intimacy!

This ideology then reflects our intimate connection to the All That Is. Only those who choose to go inward enough to experience the felt reality of the God within them really know the heart of God towards them. They know what Spirit's intention is for them. They know what God thinks of them because they are close enough for the Most High to reveal the truth of Love to them. They understand that they are not separate and apart from the very Presence that is beating their heart and is breathing them. They KNOW they are one with that very Intelligence and that their desire is also God's desire for them. That's the essence of being a "friend" of God. Some people prefer to stand on the outskirts of this Presence looking on as a mere lowly servant, posturing themselves as unworthy. The truth is you have ALWAYS been worthy, you came here worthy, you will remain worthy because there is nothing you could ever do to convince Love not to love you... to separate Itself from you. You can see this very idea being depicted through the Christ consciousness in John 15:15, when Rabbi Yeshua (Jesus) speaks to the disciples shortly before he is said to be offered up for crucifixion: "I don't call you servants anymore, because a servant doesn't know what his master is doing. But I've called you friends, because I've made KNOWN to you everything that I've heard from my Father" (International Standard Version, 2012).

In this passage, Yeshua (Jesus) calls his travel companions and protégés friends because of the knowledge and information he has shared with them. Intimacy is not relegated to romantic relationships alone. In this same way, one who stands on the outer courts of your being as a mere onlooker can't stake claim to an intimate connection with you. Intimacy isn't readily accessible to just anyone; it calls for internal connection. Intimacy is the kind of access that is not given to the common but only granted to those worthy to enter into the sacred chambers of your heart.

With Presence,

Nadia

TODAY'S THOUGHT

It's possible for you to touch someone's body but never be intimate with them if they didn't let you see the inside of their heart.

TODAY'S INTIMACY JOURNAL

Today, I found it challenging to embrace and accept intimacy

when_____

_____

_____

_____

Today, I found it easy to embrace and accept intimacy when

_____

_____

_____

_____

The key thought from Today's Chronicle I will focus on is

_____

_____

_____

_____

Purpose Chronicle, No. 5

CHANGE: THE UNAVOIDABLE ELEMENT

TODAY'S CHRONICLE FROM NADIA

Dear Former You,

Afros, natural hair, high-top fades, finger waves, wide-legged high-waisted pants, platform shoes, big gold rope chains, eyelash extensions, bell bottoms, skinny jeans, and bug-eyed shades were all considered "played out" after the era in which they began. As these fashion trends changed, you could be ridiculed for not coming current or being "with the times." Ironically, these seemingly "outdated" trends have found their way back into today's fashions. How could this be? Jean-Baptiste Alphonse Karr suggests that " the more things change, the more they stay the same."

In order for these ideas or trends to remain relevant, they had to be reinvented. As these concepts expanded, they had to be tweaked a bit, even undergo a transformation, if you will. In reality, as human beings, we aren't any different. We need change to grow. We should constantly be reinventing ourselves to stay current on our path to being our best selves. Sure, change is uncomfortable, and sometimes it even seems inconvenient. We tell ourselves how we've "always done it that way and it works," or "if it ain't broke, don't fix it." However, what we've always done IS, in fact, broken and it's no longer serving our best interest. But as fear would have it, we resist the inevitable. Fear binds us to our norm and then intimidatingly encourages us to commit to the mediocrity that our comfort zone yields. Excellence is off in the distance.

Our self-advancement is a mere mirage. In reality, we hadn't grown after all. We have only mastered our traditions and maintained our cultural norms. If we take an introspective look and recognize that we aren't progressing as we are, then why are we afraid of change? I'd submit to you that it isn't change itself that mortifies us, rather, it is trying to see ahead and picture ourselves as greater than we are right now.

We've never been the greatest version of our future self, so we have no idea what that looks or feels like. We have no real idea as to what that entails. And that's just the thing--what terrifies us is not knowing how we will maintain a greatness that we've never seen, been, or experienced. Here's a comforting truth: You already ARE who you're afraid to become. The only real change that is happening is how you will see yourself and how you will show up on the Earth.

Sometimes we are afraid of how who we are now will be viewed and received by others. They only know us as we are in this moment. So let me hand you another truth. They only know themselves as they are right now and they, too, are terrified by the idea of being anyone other than who they are right now. So don't expect them to support your growth in a way they can't support their own. And if that's the case, there's no need to be afraid of people who are just as afraid of being themselves as you are.

This is YOUR path, YOUR life, and YOUR internal work. Accept YOURSELF as you are. In this way, you'll open the portal for change to pass freely through you and for growth to take place in you exponentially. As change approaches, stay focused within yourself versus looking without yourself towards the opinions and ideas others. Your personal journey is less about another's perception of who you are and more about you coming into an awareness of self. That notion alone can be challenging, but only if you are in resistance to the process of transformation. In an effort to "go with the flow" of change, speak well of it, welcome it, and bless it as it comes. Before you know it, fear dissipates and you're well on your way to being your greatest self and being more of who and what you already are!

Embracing change,

TODAY'S THOUGHTS

The only thing that is constant is change

— HERACLITUS

Change is inevitable. It will happen with or without out you. Save yourself the stress and go with it, not against it. Don't reject it; bless it. Say to yourself "This change is the best thing for me, and I will be greater because of it!"

TODAY'S EMBRACING CHANGE JOURNAL

Today, I found it challenging to embrace change when

_____

_____

_____

_____

Today, I found it easy to embrace change when

_____

_____

_____

_____

The key thought from Today's Chronicle I will focus on is

_____

_____

_____

_____

Purpose Chronicle, No. 6

THE SCALE OF SUCCESS

The reason you want every single thing that you want, is because you think you will feel really good when you get there. But if you don't feel really good on your way to there, you can't get there. You have to be satisfied with what is while you're reaching for more.

— ABRAHAM-HICKS

Dear You,

The ideas discussed around how success is defined can simply be some of the most disheartening conversations to ever have. I've heard people say, "I'm gon' know 'I made it' when I get that Bentley." Or "why aren't things happening for me like they are for her? She got the ring, the man, the kids, the house, and the car. When am I going to be successful?" Or I've even heard, "My hustle is real! My grind is crazy! I do it so whenever I walk into a store I can buy anything I want Prada, Gucci, Fendi, and Givenchy." I find these to be really sad commentaries and thoughts, primarily because they focus on things that are perishable and tangible and, ultimately, don't give people any real internal joy or happiness.

Success isn't measured by what you live in, what you drive, what labels you wear, what's on your resume, or what's in your bank account. Success is how well you use your life to positively impact others. I've often thought, "What does success look like for me?" I have had to do some real soul-searching. I even consulted my mom, because she is one of the wisest feminine energies that I know. She's a widow to my father, a mother of five of us, a deeply spiritual woman, a warrior, and a source of strength like no other. She has always lived modestly. Before she could ever drive, she would walk, catch the city bus, or take a cab to wherever she had to go, and she taught us to do the same. My mom could take little and make much. She would cook the best meals! Most of our meals came from her being resourceful. Ironically, I'd be asking her to cook a meal I loved from my childhood in my adult life and she'd remark "Oh, child, that was a poor man's meal." Who knew?

In her early twenties, Mom started out as a college student at the University of South Carolina, Columbia, and by this time was married with three children and working full time. She eventually had to make a tough decision: her children or her. She chose her family and for her, we are her successes. She never finished that degree or became the nurse she wanted to be, but she worked for thirty-three years for the department of mental health and retired as a mental health specialist. She raised my siblings and me after my dad transitioned. She paid off her home and she is still living in it as she has been for the last thirty-five years. She paid off her vehicle as well, and it wasn't a Mercedes Benz. It was a Buick Century and she kept it for almost twenty years. My mom created consistency and stability for her family and to her she couldn't be more successful. So I asked her, "Mom, how do you measure success" and she doesn't know I wrote it all down, but here's what she said:

To be quite frank, I don't know how you MEASURE success. There is no measure for success. You set the bar for your own success. A success for one person might not necessarily be a success for somebody else. Some people set goals and they reach their pinnacle and stop, but that's a success to them. We make accomplishments every day. Whatever you want to and you do it, it's a great accomplishment. That makes it a success. Success is different steps of accomplishments. [It is] working towards something and completing [it].

Now I don't know how other people measure success but that's my take on it. Yes, you got the degree, the house, the car, the good job, the family, but is that all? Are you happy? Because if you're not, then it still isn't a success. We think society's standard is the measure, but it's about what WE want to do! People would be a lot happier if they weren't trying to reach goals set by society and just set their own goals. If you never buy a house, but you're happy, then that's good. People are killing themselves. My thing is just being happy. You have family that you love and love you—just be happy. People are under undue stress and have no quality time for the people they are struggling to support." –My mom, Wilodean R. Perry (from our phone conversation on September 13, 2016 at 2:30 pm)

I agree with my mom. What I have come to know and understand is that we have had images placed in front of us in our families, our educational arenas, our jobs, in the media and by our overall societal standards that have left an indelible impression on us. We have been sold on and persuaded by the notion that we are doing "well" if we have acquired a particular status, a certain group of friends, a certain level of education, a certain business acumen, a certain measure of wealth or material gain. We compare ourselves to other people as our gauge for how successful we are. This is what I would deem as some of the most erroneous teaching EVER.

It is gravely important to understand that each one of us was sent here into the earth for a specific mission, purpose, and work. It is something that only YOU were created to do. Even if your purpose bears some similarity to someone else's, it isn't exact in terms of the work for which YOU were sent. Even identical twins have some distinctions in their look, mannerisms, and personality...and in their SOUL. How then could we think that if we emulate what our peers, family members, co-workers, pastors and church members, leaders, and comrades have done to garner their success, that we will experience that same magnitude of "success" or feeling of fulfillment?

Have you ever been at a restaurant and weren't sure what you wanted? Couldn't figure out what you had a taste for? So you just ordered what you saw someone else order because they raved about it? You order it. It's EXCELLENT!!! But you simply weren't satisfied; it didn't hit the spot. Sure you aren't hungry anymore, but you also aren't fulfilled. Can you identify with that? I certainly can! I understand that what's perfect for the next person may not be exactly what I am looking for.

When we go along with the norm, the standard measure of success based on the "American Dream," we live this life temporarily satisfied and ultimately unfulfilled. As I scan my life and think about all of the money I've made, places I've lived, countries I've traveled to, vacations I've taken, luxury vehicles I've ridden in, the degree I have, the organizations I've been a part of. I'm convinced that these things haven't made me any more successful than a child learning how to tie his shoes. It is the people whose lives I've been able to effect change in for the better along the way that has added to improving my character and making my life more fulfilled. And it happened just from being myself. That is what brings me joy and happiness. I get to be a light to others by simply being me. That's success! I love my beautiful, abundant life! Selfless acts, unconditional love, diligent servanthood, humility, and kindness are ways that I measure how successful I am on my life's journey. I realize that I'm here in the earth to help other people discover their purpose and to help build those relationships with people when they allow me to do so. While doing that, I sometimes experience material gain, but it doesn't make me successful if I'm not impactful.

Rooting for you,

TODAY'S THOUGHT

"Success is liking yourself, liking what you do, and liking how you do it."

— MAYA ANGELOU

I'm only as successful as the people who I'm sent here to serve. I succeed when I turn on THEIR light and guide THEM towards being their best self. I choose to feel amazing about that right NOW!

TODAY'S SUCCESS JOURNAL

Today, I found it challenging to accept my success when

_____

_____

_____

_____

Today, I found it easy to accept my success when

_____

_____

_____

_____

The key thought from Today's Chronicle I will focus on is

_____

_____

_____

_____

Purpose Chronicle, No. 7

GUILT: THE PLIGHT OF THE GIVER

TODAY'S CHRONICLE FROM NADIA

Dear You,

I remember a time when I had begun to branch out into some of my own personal endeavors. I was afforded the opportunity to do some of the things that I'd always longed to do, but when the flourishing approached, it wasn't as joyous as I thought it would be. I couldn't figure out for the life of me why I wasn't enjoying what I had asked for.

It's no secret that I'm a servant at heart. I will push, encourage, support, and serve other people's dreams, goals, and ambitions. I can't even begin to tell you how fulfilling that is for me when I can help catapult someone else into their destiny. There have been times where I'd find myself being more passionate about someone else's aspirations than they were. Although, I have learned not to get so attached to others' dreams, invest more than they do, and work harder for it, I still find great joy in supporting them to the fullest extent.

As you can imagine, I approach my own ambitions, visions, and dreams with as much tenacity, if not more. I tend to, plow, fertilize, and prune my ground diligently, and then the harvest comes. I know you're probably thinking, "Well, isn't that what's supposed to happen? Where's the harm in that?" But there have been times that when my own success starts accumulating, I would somehow be riddled with guilt. I began feeling as though I'm doing something wrong or unfair, like the spotlight shouldn't be on me. It was as if it didn't belong to me although I know I sowed, asked, believed, and affirmatively prayed for it. Why didn't I think I was worth it?

I have come to understand that it is sometimes the learned plight of the giver. We know how to put out much, but we don't know how to receive. We fear what people will think because when you're a "humble servant" you aren't recognized much and you become accustomed to that way of being and doing. The moment you're being featured, highlighted, talked about in high esteem, it is unusual, and therefore, it is uncomfortable. We begin to think, "What if people think that I think too highly of myself?," "What if they think I feel I'm better than them?," or "What if I become greater and more recognized than anyone in my family?"

You know what I say to that? What if you didn't make what other people think and feel your responsibility? Instead of rehearsing stories about the feelings and thoughts of others (that YOU created by the way), let me suggest that you make a practice of scanning your own mind and heart for how YOU feel. Create the new story that it feels incredible to receive!

Sometimes the greatest among us fear being ostracized for seemingly being "too great." Abandon that illusion. It's only helping you to block the flow of blessings that are looking for you but can't find you because you are wracked with guilt. Your blessings don't have to wade through waters of inadequacy to get to you. When you decide to let go of the unworthiness and return to truth that in giving there's receiving and vice versa, your blessings will uninhibitedly flow to you. In reality, you are worthy of experiencing the same joy from yourself that you readily offer to others.

Today, I am no longer self-sabotaging, but I can admit that I did at times fear my own greatness—therein lies the root of the guilt. As I've said before, one of our greatest opponents is fear. Fear stems a myriad of deceptive emotions, including guilt, doubt, anger, frustration, jealousy and the list goes on. If I buy into it, my growth will be stunted and my goals will be paralyzed. And then what? Then fear has defeated me—with MY help! Not on my watch! Not over here in WHOLENESS! I've decided that, as Tamar Braxton said recently in an interview, "I'm worthy of all the success that comes to me."

Am I society's idea of perfect? Not by a long shot (nor am I trying to live up to that impossible mask task)! However, I Am GOD's good idea! I am giving, loving, relentless, ambitious, innovative, and creative. I am whole as my authentic self, therefore, I AM perfect as I Am.

If blessings see fit to viscously flow to me and God deems me worthy, who am I to argue with Love's generosity towards me? If you're a giver, and you've been dealing with these same feelings of guilt and the "why me" syndrome, look yourself in the mirror and make this declarative affirmation: "I AM WORTH IT!" Ultimately, it is important to understand that the greater you become, the greater the opportunities are that you can provide for someone else! The brighter your light, the more you can illuminate someone else's path! We are blessed to be a blessing! Let go of the guilt! Bask in your blessed life. Enjoy your own shine! You're here at this elevation because you're supposed to be. You absolutely belong here! Keep moving forward towards your own greatness, success, and wholeness!

With Encouragement,

Nadia

TODAY'S THOUGHT

There is just as much joy in receiving as there is in giving!

TODAY'S RELEASING GUILT JOURNAL

Today, I found it challenging to releasing guilt when

_____

_____

_____

_____

Today, I found it easy to releasing guilt when

_____

_____

_____

_____

The key thought from Today's Chronicle I will focus on is

_____

_____

_____

_____

Purpose Chronicle, No. 8

DEVELOPING FOCUS BEYOND DISTRACTIONS

My Dearest Fierce Focuser,

Sadly, MOST people DON'T know their purpose. They have no idea what they agreed to come into the physical realm to do. They aren't linked or connected with anyone who can help them uncover it. They go through life aimlessly, taking whatever is handed to them. They never really desire anything better or achieve more than the status quo.   Their entire life is one big distraction. They never fulfill their predestined purpose because they didn't even know they had one. They transition out of the physical realm without leaving behind their legacy. It's all too common--the cemetery is FULL of distracted bodies.   Sound like anybody you know? Does it sound like you? If so, it doesn't have to be!! Here's the thing: when you don't understand who you are, what you're worth, and why you're here, you have nothing to focus on or work towards. It's just that easy to give anything and everything your attention!

Think about the girl who would make a wonderful wife, mom, model, and actress. But because she doesn't KNOW her worth or purpose, she focuses only on her beauty and capitalizes on it every chance she gets. She oozes sex in her demeanor and she is confident only in her sexual prowess. She is one big promiscuous cliché, having sex with anyone who acknowledges that she is beautiful. She aborts every baby she carries and has no real concept of the nuclear makeup of a family. She never becomes who she was intended to be because she never looked inward to figure out her path and all of the endless possibilities of how she can channel her beauty.

Some people think they were born simply to die. Sure, everybody has to leave behind these physical "soul clothes." But the reality is EVERYBODY has a purpose, a reason they exist, something they are ultimately intended to do and BE! The sooner we know, fathom, dream, realize, or get the slightest inkling of what that is, we rid ourselves of the permanent state of distraction. We now have something to work towards. Although there will be times where your attention is divided, it will only be temporary.   Soon you will realize there is something bigger and greater, and you will abandon the minor distraction for the major purpose. There's NO WAY you can have a sense of the magnitude of your impact on this earth and continue in a place of lost focus! You couldn't possibly feel comfortable staying in a place of laxity and forfeiting God's plan to prosper you through your life's assignment. Now don't get me wrong, you don't have to become the world's greatest busybody who is constantly exhausting yourself with task after task in an effort to prove something to others or gain validation. I've said it before and I'll say it again, I'd rather be impactful than impressive. I'm speaking to a knowing-ness that you are here for something far more meaningful than the mundane routine of getting up every day to go to work, make money, pay bills, come home, eat dinner, shower, get back in the bed, and start it all over again in eight hours or less.

I'm talking about that thing inside of you that constantly tugs at you. You ignore it because you've convinced yourself that it's impossible, you don't know where to start, you think others are better at it or you think you'll screw up and it won't be successful. But every time you think about it, your purpose brings you so much bliss and joy. You wake up thinking about it. You think about it throughout the day. You go to bed thinking about. You've been able to naturally do it since you were a kid, and you've never been formally trained in it because it's a GIFT. THAT thing, THAT GIFT, is why you're here.

It's called a GIFT because it was given to you to give to others. It's OK to sift, sort, and find your way back to your center. Try new things. See what else you're good at. But in the grand analysis of this lifetime, it'll all divinely come back to that particular gift as the vehicle to do your purpose. You can wake up, stop avoiding it, or being distracted by unfulfilling behaviors whenever you decide. This is your wake-up call. We're all waiting on you.

Here's the truth: Everybody can BE distracted. But the only people that can STAY distracted are the ones who have no idea of their purpose, no clue about their destiny, and no interest in finding out who their greatest "self" is. In Truth we all share the common purpose of being Love in action on earth. How we choose to allow that love to be individually expressed to us is what we need to get inspired and clear about.

On purpose,

TODAY'S THOUGHT

Go inward. Seek out your purpose.
Do it. Be it. Stay focused!

TODAY'S GETTING FOCUSED JOURNAL

Today, I found it challenging to stay focused when

_____

_____

_____

_____

Today, I found it easy to stay focused when

_____

_____

_____

_____

The key thought from Today's Chronicle I will focus on is

_____

_____

_____

_____

Purpose Chronicle, No. 9

LEARNING YOUR VALUE BEYOND VALIDATION

TODAY'S CHRONICLE FROM NADIA

Dear Amazing Being,

Let's be honest--EVERYBODY wants validation!! There are people who don't need it as much, people who require it, and people who have grown accustomed to not getting it. And there isn't anyone who doesn't appreciate it when they get it. The bottom line is EVERYONE wants to be supported with words such as, "You did a great job!" "Way to go!" "You really helped me!" or "That changed my life!" There's absolutely nothing wrong with wanting confirmation that you have indeed done what you've set out to do.

Where it gets a little troubling is when that validation becomes the requirement for what you do and ultimately who you are. I can vividly remember my mom saying to me on more occasions that I can count, "Never let a man validate you." While I know she was being specific to the male gender, I have chosen to apply that wisdom to mankind as a whole. The reality is that people could see you doing well and, for one reason or another, may never decide to tell you just how well you're doing. Then what? Is all hope lost? Are you to believe that you're not who you REALLY are? Do you have no value simply because someone doesn't affirm you? Let me help you with that: you ARE what you've been waiting for!   You have to affirm yourself! It is a must that you recognize your own worth whether someone else does or not. When you are in tune with your own worth, compliments become "icing on the cake" versus the ingredients to make the cake itself. Do it for YOU! Be enough for YOU! Let your own worth be your motivation to do what you do and to be who you are. I've said it before and I'll say it again: You are WORTH it! You DESERVE it! You ARE MORE THAN ENOUGH—FOR YOU!

In Confidence,

Nadia

TODAY'S THOUGHT

Never let a man validate you!

—MY MOMMA

TODAY'S SELF-VALUE JOURNAL

Today, I found it challenging to value myself when

_____

_____

_____

_____

Today, I found it easy to value myself when

_____

_____

_____

_____

The key thought from Today's Chronicle I will focus on is

_____

_____

_____

_____

Part Four:
The World
Chronicles

World Chronicle, No. 1: Trusting God And Others

TODAY'S CHRONICLE FROM NADIA

Dear You,

How does The Creator feel about all this trust we have in Him? Is it too much to handle? Is it overwhelming that millions of us are trusting this Infinite Presence all at once? Isn't it too much pressure? OF COURSE NOT! This speaks to the vastness of how GREAT God is. But if we are made in the image and likeness of the Most High, why aren't human beings deemed equally as trustworthy? I mean seriously, have you ever thought about that? What makes us readily say, "I trust God," who we have never physically seen? Likewise, we resort to saying with the same vehemence, "I don't trust people" even though we have experienced people on this physical plane. But is this even possible? I'm not here to confuse your theology at all. As a matter of fact, this isn't even about religion. This is a challenge to think about the ideals surrounding trust and how we determine who is worthy and unworthy.

Let's consider a few things about trust. Take a moment to think about the truth of how love and trust can be synonymous in many instances. Typically, if we say we trust someone, we somehow associate that with loving that individual. We trust them because we love them, and we love them because we can trust them. They have in some way displayed characteristics, behaviors, deeds, or acts toward us that deems them trustworthy in our eyes. Right? The same way we determine that we trust God, right?

But what happened before you ever knew to DISTRUST someone? You just trusted them, right? It wasn't until you lived a little and figured out that some people just aren't honest, dependable, or reliable that the lack of trust formed. It is safe to say that our experiences with trust shape our perception of what trust is to us.

But was the purpose of those untrustworthy beings entering your life to cause you to become bitter, cold, unloving, and distrusting of every living thing? Probably not! I'd suggest that they came into your space to teach you lessons about you. I would dare say that they came into your life to help you awaken to your strengths and weaknesses and create standards that lift you from ignorance to enlightenment.

Let me eliminate any ambiguity and sum it up for you: Our personal relationships are often a reflection of our spiritual relationship with God. As it is above, so it is below. How did we find out whether or not we could trust God? We trusted Him! As Thrall, McNicol, and Lynch wrote in their book TrueFaced, "God couldn't help us until we trusted Him with who we really were."

If I were to be completely honest, I may find it difficult to trust when I don't KNOW who or what I'm trusting. Even if I've had several opportunities to build a rapport with you, all I can really know about you is what you offer, reveal, or project. It would take real intimacy to know someone (I expounded on this in Purpose Chronicle No. 4). But I also can't know you any more than I know myself. Unfortunately, most of our "selves" are made up of societal imprints, social norms, and constructs. We're also imprinted by the culture of our family, ethnic groups, and religions. All these ideas define us, and we conform to what's expected—ergo our inability to know, experience and share our truest self. We are a mere representation of the sum total of other people's expectations of us. Trust me (no pun intended), I've done it as well and it's the most uncomfortable existence I've ever lived. Too often, people have sent out their representative who is clearly wearing a "please everybody" mask. Therefore, no one knows who you REALLY are, and in reality, neither do YOU! And we wonder why we are having difficulty trusting others!?!

Consider this: Sometimes we don't trust OTHER people because ultimately we don't KNOW ourselves well enough to trust OURSELVES. I can't trust YOU anymore than I can trust ME. In a society where going against the grain is deemed rebellious, we'd rather not rock the boat and be authentic. We're afraid to remove our masks because we don't want to be judged. We fear that if people knew the little that we do know about ourselves, they wouldn't love us quite the same--or at all. So we live in the constant secret torment and fear that comes from not knowing what people think about us, what they may feel if they had certain information about us, or if they can handle all of the "stuff" that comes with our being authentically real with them. This conformity to people pleasing is the beginning of a stifling life and the end of any form of peace.

Fear and mask wearing are now and will always be counterproductive to faith, love, truth, and trust. Just know that you don't have to choose that imprisoned life for yourself where you are locked up with the images of other people's truth for you. Free yourself!! You are made in the very image of the Source. You, too, are a creator so create the life you want to live. Create the energies you will attract simply because you are choosing to be better. We are all reflections of each other. So if you are encountering beings on your path that you deem untrustworthy, that is your opportunity to do some introspection and find out what is it that's inside of you that is now showing up outside of you. Maybe it's not them— maybe they are reflecting you.

I challenge you to get up each day, go to the mirror, refuse to be anything other than your truest self, and speak to yourself everything that you are and affirm what you want to be. Remind yourself of everything that God is and remember that that is also who you are. Don't live beneath that, live AS that. When you begin to show up that way in the world (loving, giving, kind, joyful, authentic, confident, peaceable, trustworthy) then others who reflect the Creator as you do will show up in your life. I'm not referring to just churchgoing people, or pious, religious, self-righteous folks. I'm speaking of people who have evidence that they bear God's spirit. The Love beings who have compassion and understanding for all you are all you are not and all you are becoming.

As I observe that thought, I'm reminded of these particular passages in I John 4. Let's observe verses 1, 12, 13, 20, and 21of the English Standard Version of the bible:

> *1 Beloved, do not believe every spirit, but test the spirits, whether they are of God; because many false prophets have gone out into the world.*

> *12 No one has seen God at any time. If we love one another, God abides in us, and His love has been perfected in us.*

> *13 By this we know that we abide in Him, and He in us, because He has given us of His Spirit No one has ever seen God; if we love one another, God abides in us and his love is perfected in us.*

> *20 If anyone says, "I love God," and hates his brother, he is a liar; for he who does not love his brother whom he HAS seen, how can he love God whom he has NOT seen?*

> *21 And this commandment we have from Him: that he who loves God must love his brother also.*

Trust me,

Nadia

TODAY'S THOUGHT

Loving and trusting yourself first makes it that much easier to love and trust others.

TODAY'S LEARNING TO TRUST GOD JOURNAL

Today, I found it challenging to learn to trust God when

_____

_____

_____

_____

Today, I found it easy to learn to trust God when

_____

_____

_____

_____

The key thought from Today's Chronicle I will focus on is

_____

_____

_____

_____

World Chronicle, No. 2: The Institution Of Family

There is no such thing as a 'broken family. Family is family, and it is not determined by marriage certificates, divorce papers, and adoption documents. Families are made in the heart. The only time family becomes null is when those ties in the heart are cut. If you cut those ties, those people are not your family. If you make those ties, those people are your family. And if you hate those ties, those people will still be your family because whatever you hate will always be with you.

— C. JOYBELL C.

Dear You,

I am not traditional in any sense of the word, therefore my family is not traditional, either. I have blood relatives who don't know me beyond seeing me as a kid, some whom I've yet to meet, some who may not even know my middle name, and some who don't know any deeper qualities about me other than what they can see at face value or on social media. I consider those persons my relatives. We haven't quite established the connection that may deem us "family." However, I respect them and I love them as The Spirit would have me do.

Nevertheless, there are some blood-related family members that feel a sense of entitlement to you or whatever you have simply because they have the position of a family member. They may know the visible exterior details about you, but they never took a real interest in building a relationship with you. Despite this absence of authentic connection, somehow they have adopted the notion that you will engage them in a way that suggests that there's an intimate bond or you'll extend to them the loyalty that they believe goes with the territory of their title. In their opinion, you owe it to them whether they nurture a relationship with you or not!

On the converse, there are also instances where we inherit family members by way of marriage, either our own or by way of someone marrying into our family. Daughter-in-laws become more like daughters. Son-in-laws become more like sons. Some people rename their mother-in-law "mother-in-love" because the bond extends beyond legal law to the more powerful law of love. Families have all types of unique dynamics that bear no need of explanation, judgment, or comparison. No one being gets to determine for the next individual who can be considered "family."

Families can consist of whatever we draw into our experience as the tribe we desire. Families can have two mommies or two daddies. Families can have parents of contrasting ethnic backgrounds with multi-ethnic children. Families can have parents with adopted children reflecting the same or varying ethnic backgrounds or nationalities. Families can embody such a loving presence that they allow Infinity Loving Presence to guide them to a child who they can sense is void of the awareness of love's abundance. They can decide to take them in and be that very love to that child. We see this very act depicted in the film The Blind Side where Leigh Anne (Sandra Bullock) and her husband, Sean, (Tim McGraw) take in Michael (Quinton Aaron), a homeless teenager whose biological family had succumb to poverty and the misuse of drugs. It is evident as the movie progresses that Michael had rarely experienced the kind of love, warmth, protection, attention, and quality time that was readily available in the Tuohy family. Love called them to action. That very love propelled Michael into showing up and operating as his best self.

In my experience, I have learned that family isn't just about the nuclear makeup of mom, dad, siblings, grandparents, aunts, uncles, cousins, nieces, and nephews. We don't have the luxury of choosing those who are related to us via DNA. We aren't even always able to make a genuine connection with those who are considered our biological family.

I love EVERYONE!! But I'm most fond of my friends and family who have taken the time to know the heart of me and invested their love energy in building a relationship with me that resulted in an undeniable heart connection. MY family is made up of people whose love is unselfish, has no limits and no boundaries, loves me with my flaws and all, supports me, corrects me in love, seeks to understand me, doesn't envy me, encourages me, and respects me whether or not they agree with me or my choices. We may not all have the same blood running through our veins, but we have the same heart to love unconditionally!

In the Spirit of Family,

TODAY'S THOUGHT

Family is birthed out of the heart and blood couldn't make them any closer.

TODAY'S FINDING FAMILY JOURNAL

Today, I found it challenging to find and accept the spirit of

family when_____

_____

_____

_____

Today, I found it easy to find and accept the spirit of family

when_____

_____

_____

_____

The key thought from Today's Chronicle I will focus on is

_____

_____

_____

_____

World Chronicle, No. 3: The Art Of Marriage

Dear You,

Many of us are on this quest for a perfect partnership. We treat marriage like it's a one-person show. We fail to realize that a marriage is made of two people. Marriage consists of two flawed beings who must be committed to constantly doing self-improvement in order to grow personally and collectively. In this way, the marriage gets better when YOU get better.

The marriage breaks down when you're not invested in your personal wholeness.

We accepted society's notion that partnership is fifty-fifty. Religion has added to that notion that two halves then become one, creating the whole. Mathematically speaking, this idea would be correct. However, in partnership, fifty-fifty refers to divorce terms, and if you want your marriage to work then it's not about splitting everything up. A successful marriage will require 100% of each person. It's about bringing all of you to the table and giving it all you've got as you consistently move towards your wholeness.

But what DO you bring to the table?

Do you bring traditional thoughts, ideas, judgment, criticism, unrealistic expectations, and fairytale ideas? Do you bring your long list of must-haves, do's and don'ts? Are you comparing your partner to the many love stories you've seen, read, and heard about from books, movies, friends, or by watching your parents? Are you comparing your mate to yourself?

There is no perfect mold for marriage. Marriage is clay and we create it, shape it, and customize it based on the needs, wants, and desires of the two people involved. All too often, we are looking to marry ourselves. We start describing our ideal mate and, more often than not, we are describing who we are. We constantly experience disappointment because we are expecting from someone something they have never demonstrated they were capable of—Being YOU!

Having things in common and sharing in core values is key to compatibility, but sameness and exactness shouldn't be required. Allow room for differences. Learn to accept others as they are and give them room to grow. Remember, your partner is a reflection of you. Don't expect something from them that you aren't willing to give. Don't make them feel as though you are the standard and they have to work to be like you. In those times when you find yourself frustrated with all that you think they aren't, consider your inadequacies and the patience and compassion you'll need to be extended to you for all that you aren't. Always be careful how you speak about them to others when you do become frustrated.

Be mindful who you choose as a sounding board. In particular, don't share your marriage challenges to miserable people. For the sake of this point, let me define my idea of miserable people. These are people who are wretchedly unhappy, unreasonably melancholy, despondently bitter, faithfully heartbroken, pitifully ungrateful, covetously sad, and pathetically complacent. This specifically includes folks who are unhappily married, bitterly divorced, disdainfully single, unable to maintain a stable relationship, never had a real partnership, married for convenience, settled for less, never been married, home-wreckers, those who prefer to have you share in their non-existent love life, and those who cringe when they see others reconcile amicably. My point is—Don't take relationship advice from MISERABLE people.

One of the best things you can do for your marriage is to keep outside parties—outside. Keep their opinions low on the totem pole of importance. Keep their extraneous commentary out of your dinner conversations and pillow talk. It is not imperative that your spouse knows how your confidant views them, especially when you are only sharing your perspective with your friend or trusted confidant. Create loving boundaries for your family so they don't take the liberty to overstep and dishonor your relationship in any way. Don't forget that you are crafting this picture of your marriage in the mind of others with what you choose to disclose and share.

I'm not saying you have to be a prisoner to your union if there is something unsafe happening. In that case, pursue the RIGHT help IMMEDIATELY. Nevertheless, keep in mind that the agreement was made with you and your partner, not everyone else. Whether it's an open marriage, a polyamorous marriage, a traditional two-person marriage, a polygamous marriage, a heterosexual marriage, a same gender-loving marriage, or a marriage not bound by law, it's the marriage you agreed to. You don't owe anyone an explanation, an apology, or a regular update on your marital affairs. Surround your marriage with loving speech, loving ideas, and loving and supportive beings.

Remember to show up in the marriage. It is not one partner's responsibility to manage all areas of the union. If you're good at it, take the initiative to do it. Don't wait on permission or approval. Do it because it's your contribution to creating the flow of ease and effortlessness in your marriage. Take time to learn your partner's love languages and implement them. Remember to communicate about EVERYTHING. If you need more or less of something, tell your partner. They can't read your mind no matter how telepathic you think they are. If you like what they do, let them know. Don't just complain, encourage. Always say, "Thank you." Don't take anything they do for granted. They don't owe you anything. Gratitude will breed more abundance.

Be open to change and evolution personally and collectively with your partner. If you and your spouse are committed to your individual growth, then expect that the person you met at twenty-five will not be the same being at thirty-five. Be supportive and understanding. And finally, as my marriage taught me, remember YOU! Don't sacrifice your self-love and internal love to extend external love to someone else.

The more you love you and show up for you, the greater your capacity to love others.

With Wisdom,

Nadia

TODAY'S THOUGHT

Marriage is a partnership that works best when you are present, aware of yourself, and show up fully to contribute to the overall health of the relationship.

TODAY'S THE ART OF MARRIAGE JOURNAL

Today, I found it challenging to accept the beauty of marriage

when_____

_____

_____

_____

Today, I found it easy to accept the beauty of marriage when

_____

_____

_____

_____

The key thought from Today's Chronicle I will focus on is

_____

_____

_____

_____

World Chronicle, No. 4: Be Your Community

TODAY'S CHRONICLE FROM NADIA

Hey My Loves,

When you hear the word community, what comes to mind? In my experience, most people think of a neighborhood, a subdivision, a particular ethnic group, or feeding or donating to the less fortunate. Although these are all areas of community and service in some form, they are not all encompassing. Well, what is community then? Community has a literal definition, but keep in mind that you also get to help define what community is really all about because it starts with you! By definition, community is a group of people with diverse characteristics who are linked by social ties, share common perspectives, and engage in joint action in geographical locations or settings. In essence, you find ways to commune with those whom you have things in common. Commune is the base word of communication and community. To commune is to share one's intimate thoughts or feelings with someone or something. To sum it up, a community is a group of people with likenesses, commonalities, and shared ideals or goals. They are a group of people who share the same issues, concerns, burdens, and convictions. They are people who come together in the same place at the same time for the same cause to participate in an exchange about what they share in common and how it can be used for a greater good.

"Well, when you say it like that, Nadia, I know of lots of

communities." PRECISELY! Communities are everywhere! They aren't limited to our subdivisions and neighborhoods, our churches or sororities, our clubs and organizations, or our religious sects. You can create the community that appeals to YOU. But you can't wait for it to come to you. If we all is sit around lackadaisically, expecting some random person to come and draft us out of our seclusion into their prominent group, how will the community we long for ever be created? If you were thinking that, I encourage you to THINK AGAIN!

If you're looking for positivity—BE IT!

If you're looking to link up with a community of cancer survivors—CREATE IT!

If you're looking for a different kind of support for your culture—DEVELOP IT!

If you're looking for a positive, unity-promoting environment that is culturally diverse—BUILD IT!

If you're looking for a community of people living with HIV/AIDS who won't shun you—FORM IT!

If you are in need of a community who proudly celebrates who you are and won't judge you based on who you love—BECOME IT!

If you are you a single mom, a musician, an athlete, a pastor, a minister, a carpenter, a racecar driver, an ex-convict reformed, a singer, a baker, a cook, a seamstress, a coach, or an author and there is no place for you to link up your ideas, gifts, and talents--then YOU BECOME the community you want and need!! You ARE your community! It starts with YOU! Right now, someone is looking for you just like you're looking for them. So what are YOU going to do about it?

In Service,

TODAY'S THOUGHT

BE the change you want to see.

— MAHATMA GANDHI

TODAY'S JOY IN COMMUNITY JOURNAL

Today, I found it challenging to find the joy in community

when_____

_____

_____

_____

Today, I found it easy to find the joy in community when

_____

_____

_____

_____

The key thought from Today's Chronicle I will focus on is

_____

_____

_____

_____

World Chronicle, No. 5: This Isn't A Competition!

My Dear Confident Love,

Have you ever had a conversation with a friend and you're sharing some of your victories and it seems like everything you have done, this friend has done it too—and ten times better if you let them tell it? At first, you try not to resort to thinking that the friend is doing any tit for tat comparing and competing. Then you sense that maybe, YOU'RE being a bit of a braggart and should dumb down your excitement. You reason that maybe YOU are making your friend feel uncomfortable, small, or not as accomplished as you are. You eventually decide that maybe you shouldn't share your successes at all! Your friend isn't as excited for you as you thought they would be. In all actuality, the friend is a little green with envy, and is a bit intimidated by your running list of achievements. This wasn't your intent at all! To avoid feeling like you're doing something insensitive, you totally retreat and, going forward, you are reluctant to share any details of your happiness.

But don't you deserve to be genuinely happy about doing well without feeling like you're hurting someone? Shouldn't you be able to tell your news to trusted friends without fear of offending them with your well-being? The answer is an emphatic, resounding "YES!" You simply CANNOT go through life apologizing for other people's insecurities. YOU are your greatest competition! Don't engage in meaningless competition with people who should really be supporters. To those that compete and compare out of jealousy, consider this advice from Jennifer James:

Jealousy is simply and clearly the fear that you do not have value. Jealousy scans for evidence to prove the point—that others will be preferred and rewarded more than you. There is only one alternative—self-value. If you cannot love yourself, you will not believe that you are loved. You will always think it's a mistake or luck. Take your eyes off others and turn the scanner within. Find the seeds of your jealousy, clear the old voices and experiences. Put all the energy into building your personal and emotional security. Then you will be the one others envy, and you can remember the pain and reach out to them.

To those of you who shrink back because of the jealous, competitive nature of others, here's my advice--give yourself permission to be happy for yourself and other's successes. There is no shortage of success. There is MORE than enough to go around! Feel comfortable with your own power without fearing or worrying that your success will hurt others.

With Confidence,

TODAY'S THOUGHT

Those that genuinely love you will ALWAYS celebrate your success. They will not find ways to compete with you out of their own lack of confidence.

TODAY'S RELEASING JEALOUSY JOURNAL

Today, I found it challenging to release jealousy when

_____

_____

_____

_____

Today, I found it easy to release jealousy when

_____

_____

_____

The key thought from Today's Chronicle I will focus on is

_____

_____

_____

_____

World Chronicle, No. 6: We're Not Accepting Applications For Enemies

Hey Friend!

I have resolved that I have NO enemies. I know you're saying to yourself, "You must be crazy! Everybody has enemies!" I'm going to shoot twelve-gauge sized bullet holes in that theory! I have NO enemies! If I have enemies, I know nothing about them because I didn't create them. They have hired and employed themselves, but I refuse to put them on the payroll. I didn't send out enemy applications. I didn't host an enemy job fair. I didn't post any enemy job openings. If they are an enemy, it's because they want to be. If I have enemies, I would love to hear how they became my enemy and what logic they used to determine they should be against me. I'd be most interested in knowing who they are and how they strategize because their plots and schemes are an epic failure to me.

My mom always said to me, "You will talk to anybody, and you've been that way since you were old enough to talk." And guess what? I'm still that way! I'll even know people don't like me and STILL speak to them because I'm clear that I have given them no reason to dislike, hate, or be against me. I refuse to engage in their enemy behavior!

I speak to them, embrace them, love them, and recruit them into a loving experience. If you can identify with the energy I'm speaking to, you can probably conclude that you don't have any enemies either. Rather, you have dedicated admirers that WANT to hate you but can't really justify why they want to oppose, hate, or dislike you. I've learned that when people know that you're unaffected by their dislike of you, the only option they're left with is to respect you for being consistent. But, I don't take it personally--I take it spiritually. When a person is bewildered by their own dislike of another person and say, "I don't know WHY I don't like her or him, I just DON'T!" that is a clear indication to me that they are merely having an internal conflict. It is happening INSIDE of them. It's not even about you!

Whatever its origin, this imbalance creates feelings of insecurity and inadequacy so much so that when this being is confronted with a presence they'd much rather have, it frustrates them and spawns discontentment. The discontentment is not specific to a person as much as it is with self. The moment an individual gives ear to the insecure internal dialogue, they are convinced that what they are feeling is happening outside of them from a particular individual.

As love beings, it is our responsibility to be aware of each other and respond in the way we would like for someone to react to us when we are at war with ourselves. It is no secret my beloved¬—you have no enemies. All of your enemies are simply by-products of the fear in your mind. Your fear wants to disarm you of your spiritual awareness and ammunition and invite you into battle you were never intended to lose. What is the battle about? It's about victoriously conceding to our self-worth and seeing ourselves the same way we are being held in thought in the Divine Mind. The more aware we become of ourselves, who we are, WHOSE we are, and what we are worthy of, our stride in the race of life becomes more confident. As we do our internal work to tear down our own and others' misconceptions, we begin to reflect and demonstrate that very healing in the world. In turn, our connections with others will also reflect that same love and healing.

Victoriously,

Nadia

TODAY'S THOUGHT

Don't war with yourself. Know yourself. Love yourself. Heal yourself. See yourself as you were created to be— Perfect, Whole and Complete.

TODAY'S NO ENEMIES JOURNAL

Today, I found it challenging to accept that I have no enemies

when_____

_____

_____

_____

Today, I found it easy to accept that I have no enemies when

_____

_____

_____

_____

The key thought from Today's Chronicle I will focus on is

_____

_____

_____

_____

World Chronicle, No. 7: Forgiveness Is An Inside Job

TODAY'S CHRONICLE FROM NADIA

Hey My Shugah!

Seriously, Forget about it! I am of the belief that trust and forgiveness are not synonymous! The mere fact that you have chosen to free yourself and the offender from the wrong that has been done doesn't mean you have to resume the previous trust that had been established in that connection. This also applies to your relationship with yourself. You are not obligated to return to your former state of being once you forgive yourself. Hopefully from the point of resolution with self, you will expand, evolve, and grow. Once your trust has been violated, it should be a process of rebuilding over time. It would simply be foolish to believe you could pick up where you left off. This is only one side of the forgiveness coin.

On the flip side of it, let's talk about what forgiveness means. Now, there are several ways that forgiveness can be viewed. The perspective that I have chosen to adopt indicates that love and forgiveness are inextricably tied. You can't have one without the other! The parallel to this perspective is that it is equally important to learn how to forget. I didn't exactly pull this forgiveness model out of thin air. I took the suggestion from a passage of scripture (1 Corinthians 13:5) that notes, "Love keeps no record of wrong (resentment). Another translation reads: "Love keeps no record of BEING wronged."

Now don't get me wrong! I'm not suggesting that you be superhuman and not feel the pain, resentment, frustration, and anger that sometimes comes with the territory of the offense. By all means, feel your feelings. I'm just saying make a conscious decision to NOT constantly torture yourself by daily revisiting the place of pain. That behavior is counterproductive to your healing. If you're going to stay stuck in the time capsule of pain and continually experiencing what already happened, you may as well hang up your forgiveness shoes and be plain old unforgiving!

What I understand the most about the difficulty of forgetting is that it can be all about WHO caused you the pain. The closer they are to your heart, sometimes, the deeper the wound. The people closest to you seemingly have the ability to hurt you the most because we tend to trust them the most. I've trusted people with my most valuable parts, such as my gift to sing. Singing is a gift that I have presented before thousands, nationally and internationally. However, it is a gift that at one point I had come to despise. I found myself feeling inadequate because of an incident where I was openly humiliated and ridiculed in front of my singing peers for a mistake I made in a song. It scarred me for years and I became very insecure about my singing to the point of being overly critical of myself and afraid to sing for fear that I'd make a mistake. I lost my desire to sing altogether! It wasn't until recently that I found my voice again. I came to realize that I needed to forgive MYSELF for not being someone else's idea of perfect. I allowed the negative judgment of my most trusted singing peers to create in me these unrealistic expectations of myself, and although I had forgiven the offense, I had not released myself from the sting of the memory. I loved and respected these people so much that their ridicule became what validated my ability to deliver excellence when I sang. It never dawned on me to just forget about it! I never considered simply encouraging myself with the truth, which is that even the most skilled person is capable of making a mistake! I'm not without flaw and TODAY I forgive myself for expecting something of myself that not even God expects. Today I erase the record I was replaying of this incident that kept the lie alive! Today, I realize they had no idea that what they did in jest was stifling to the use of my gift. Today, I CHOOSE to forget about it and go on to do what I'm gifted, skilled, and purposed to do by being my BEST ME!

With a heart of forgiveness,

TODAY'S THOUGHT

*Forgiveness is an option you can't afford
to not choose, and forgetting is an ability
that you can't afford not to exercise.*

TODAY'S SELF-FORGIVENESS JOURNAL

Today, I found it challenging to forgive myself when

_____

_____

_____

_____

Today, I found it easy to forgive myself when

_____

_____

_____

_____

The key thought from Today's Chronicle I will focus on is

_____

_____

_____

_____

World Chronicle, No. 8: Your Perception, Your Truth

Dear You,

Things aren't always as they seem. Perception is all about the pair of eyes that view it and the mind that processes it. The mind forms an opinion and comes to a conclusion based on the experience of that individual. So if perception is individually based, can one person be wrong and the other right? Not at all! It isn't about who is right or wrong as the ego would have us believe. It's more so about an awareness of the original intent of what we are viewing. One person may be completely out of alignment but not wrong for seeing things differently. On the other hand, the person who processes things a little differently may be right in sync with the original perspective of the idea or "thing." " There can be as many perceptions of one "thing" as there are people.

To create a visual for you let's say someone literally fills a glass midway with a liquid, and then asks several different people "is the glass half empty or half full?" There is no right or wrong answer. There are simply several ways of looking at it, viewing it, and perceiving it. Did the person fill the cup to the brim and then drink it or pour down to halfway? Did they fill it only halfway to begin with? Only the person who poured the drink would know how it was done originally. However, with the information given, you can perceive it however you'd like. Some might say that the pessimistic view is that it's half empty. Others might argue that the optimists would see it as half full. That is where it's appropriate to say "to each his own" as opposed to getting into a senseless debate of opinion.

With perception, you often have to pick and choose your battles. Can you imagine the back-and-forth debates of perception as the Bible and other religious literature and materials were being compiled? According to my sources over at Christianity-Stack Exchange, "The common consensus is that the writing of the books of the Bible began sometime after 1500 BC, and concluded prior to 100 AD. This would be a period of about 1600 years." Now you know like I know that anything that takes 1600 years to compile had varied interpretations, differences of opinions, and different perceptions about how it all went down. That reason alone keeps me from arguing the Bible with anyone! All are entitled to their opinions and perceptions—the Bible is full of them. I think what's most important to do is to hold fast to your convictions and be governed by the things that most accurately reflect YOU, and never expect for another person's convictions to be yours. That would then make YOU the standard--the type of standard that all of us are too flawed to be. In all things just remember that respect is paramount. Keep in the forefront of your mind that love is the more excellent way in any circumstance and that sameness is not required for love. I can respect you AND love you even if I don't agree with you—even if we don't share the same truth, perspective, or perception. You reserve the right to create your own reality and, therefore, live in your own truth. Once we align in THAT truth of respect, unconditional love, and oneness, we experience real harmony.

Truthfully and harmoniously,

Nadia

TODAY'S THOUGHTS

To thine own self be true!

—WILLIAM SHAKESPEARE VIA
JOHNIFER Q. FASHION

*Live in your own truth while
respecting another's right to
do the same!*

TODAY'S CHANGING PERCEPTION JOURNAL

Today, I found it challenging to change my perception when

_____

_____

_____

_____

Today, I found it easy to change my perception when

_____

_____

_____

_____

The key thought from Today's Chronicle I will focus on is

_____

_____

_____

_____

World Chronicle, No. 9: Can You Handle The Truth?

Hi My Darlings!

We all can remember that poignant moment in the film "A Few Good Men" where the TRUTH was unveiled. Under heavy pressure from Lieutenant Kaffee (Tom Cruise), and unnerved by being caught in one of his own lies, Colonel Jessep (Jack Nicholson) furiously declares, "You can't handle the truth!" Although Colonel Jessep was caught in an untruth, I agree that sometimes people can't handle the truth they are probing for so deeply. For the most part, I'm an open book when I feel my personal truths can be helpful to others. Some truths I volunteer, other truths I delay until people seek them out and are brazen enough to ask. Should someone in my life demand, "Tell me the truth!" I will respect their courage enough to let them have the truth they're looking for and feel they can handle.

But when I discern that people are merely meddling and don't have honest intentions when prodding me for a truth they want, I take the position that I learned from my Godmother, Earthia Jenkins, by asking, "What are you going to do with that information?" If you feel justified in nosing around to uncover my personal business, then I have the right to know how you will be using that information that you probably can't handle in the first place. That wisdom-filled approach is called discretion!   I'm always ready, willing, available, and honest enough to tell you the truth. However, I have had enough life experiences to know that boundaries have to be established in order to safeguard my private life. It's really simple. Everyone shouldn't be privy to the dark corners in every chamber of your heart. You should be mindful about giving public access to private doors unless it is a tool for healing others.

You don't have to walk around in constant paranoia, looking over your shoulder, and suspecting that everyone means you harm. On the other hand, you can't assume that everyone you encounter has your best interest at heart and readily make them your most trusted confidant. Pouring your heart out to anyone and everyone who has time to listen only leaves you feeling vulnerable, easily susceptible to hurt, and ultimately feeling like a victim of sorts. Until you have spent enough time learning the character of a man or woman, be discreet. If it is a "truth" that you aren't in worry of being repeated, then share away! But if you get the slightest notion that someone can't handle the weight of your truth, keep your mouth shut! That is also called discretion.

You might ask, "So does that make me fake or dishonest?" NO. That makes you wise. Wisdom will make the difference between you and the person who ends up victimized by their own hand.

In all honesty,

Nadia

TODAY'S THOUGHT

It stands to reason that if I don't learn to use wisdom in how and what to disclose, I could end up being my own predator and a victim of my own naiveté.

TODAY'S ACCEPTING THE TRUTH JOURNAL

Today, I found it challenging to accept the truth when

_____

_____

_____

_____

Today, I found it easy to accept the truth when

_____

_____

_____

_____

The key thought from Today's Chronicle I will focus on is

_____

_____

_____

_____

Part Five: The Legacy Chronicles

Legacy Chronicle, No. 1: Developing Servant Leadership

Dear Selfless One,

It is my personal belief that every notable and praiseworthy leader is first the chief of servants! All leaders should be servants first and there should be no two ways about it. It's simple: Don't require anything of your team that you aren't willing to first BE.   If you have an organization, business, or religious following, feel free to adopt this leadership model that I've created for my businesses and organizations:

NADIA'S BUSINESS RULES

We are all important. There are no big "I's", little "you's", lofty titles, or leaders whose dreams and visions are being served by others. We are all leaders AND servants. The greatest among us is also the least among us. We are one body and one movement with one purpose and many gifts. We are all headed in the same upward direction, and we serve the needs of all people.

We are not a cult. We do not manipulate people into doing anything by maintaining control over them, brainwashing them to believe our tenets, or proclaiming to be superior to all other movements. We all have the option of being here and choosing what to believe. We are all in charge of our own destiny. We are all provided with the same information and we can choose how and when to use it.

We are not a sorority, fraternity, or gang. We do not initiate, jump in, or haze anyone in order to gain entry into our organization. We do not require anyone to give a specific amount of money in order to serve. There are no negative consequences for not giving a specific amount to the organization.

We are all brothers and sisters. We are all are treated equally and respectfully. We are all here of our own free will and like hearts to serve others. We are here of our own free will with like hearts to serve others. We do not find it necessary to know the intimate details of anyone's life as a prerequisite to serve, nor do we desire to micromanage such details.

We all respect that each person's relationship with God is PERSONAL. It does not warrant scrutiny. We are here to love ALL, reach ALL, and serve ALL in a non-judgmental, non-threatening, non-intimidating environment that doesn't discriminate or ostracize anyone. ALL are welcome to develop their gifts in a safe, learning environment and use those matured gifts to serve others.

We are servant leaders. We are all great within our own right. NO ONE, I repeat, NO ONE is to BE served as a deity. We are here to serve the lives, purposes, and dreams of OTHERS, not merely our own!   We are not here to serve in order to be seen or to get rich. Wealth does follow service, but money and notoriety is neither our motivation nor our goal.

According to Blanchard and Hodges in their book The Servant Leader, there are some distinct differences between the self-serving leader and the servant leader. One of the most notable differences is how each respective leader responds to feedback. They note that the self-serving leader will respond negatively to feedback in an effort to further protect his status or ego while the servant leader will welcome the feedback to improve on the service he provides. The servant leader sees leadership as an act of service.

The authors also distinguish between self-serving and servant leadership by their approach to creating a succession plan. Blanchard and Hodges define these distinctions as follows:

"Self-serving leaders (who are addicted to power, recognition, and who are afraid of loss of position) are not likely to spend any time or effort training their replacements. Servant leaders (who consider their position as being on loan and as an act of service) look beyond their own season of leadership and prepare the next generation of leaders."

The authors also outline many other enlightening notions to include Change, Valuing People and Performance, The Four Leadership Styles, and my personal favorite, Accountability Relationships. I suggest you go and grab this literary treasure. However, I'll share this final nugget from the book with you.

Let's face it--as leaders, we can sometimes live under the guise that we have all of the answers. There's a hierarchy in whatever our particular business or organization model is, and we are under pressure to be the answer, the problem solver, or the Olivia Pope for our team. But who tells us the truth about how well we're leading or not? Who is willing to be painfully honest with us about ourselves? Whose advice and wisdom did we undervalue, and because we refused to listen, we were left to our own foolish devices? How often are we candid enough with our team in telling them the truth about our errors, our areas that need improvement, or the necessary corrections they helped us to make?

Blanchard and Hodges suggest that we all need truth tellers in our lives to help keep us on track. In fact, they write that having them in our lives is probably our "greatest opportunity for growth." They recommend that it be someone who isn't directly affected by what we do. The authors regard feedback as a gift, and they note that when a self-serving leader kills the messenger, they cut off their access to those gems of wisdom.

Ultimately, people want to know that they can trust you as a leader. They want to know that you value them. They want to know that they can be honest with you about how you can improve without fear of negative backlash. They also want to know that you are practical and human, which will be evident in you being honest about your challenges as a leader. They want to know that you can become as they are--THE SERVANT.

With Servitude,

Nadia

TODAY'S THOUGHTS

A servant leader never asks anyone to do something they wouldn't be willing to do themselves.

– BLANCHARD AND HODGES

If you're ever going to be a leader who has integrity, you must first learn how to SERVE with integrity! Demonstrate to others what you expect from them.

TODAY'S SERVANTHOOD JOURNAL

Today, I found it challenging to embrace servanthood when

_____

_____

_____

_____

Today, I found it easy to embrace servanthood when

_____

_____

_____

The key thought from Today's Chronicle I will focus on is

_____

_____

_____

_____

Legacy Chronicle, No. 2: Be Transformed

It Is Not Selfish To Do
What Is Best For You

—MARK SUTTON

Dear New You,

Let go. Release all things that no longer serve you, such as, old thoughts, habits, feelings, stresses, fears, doubts, anxieties, worries, frustrations, practices, routines, pathologies, patterns, friends, foes, and even family. If it doesn't benefit your best self, then it hinders you and perpetuates your lack of growth. If you're OK with not moving forward and being stagnant, then change nothing! If you recognize that you allow these things and people to impede the free flow of loving energy into your experience, change should not be optional! It's not that "something's GOTTA give"--the reality is something WILL give or break down! The good news is you get to choose to keep the toxins that "dis-ease" your being OR emancipate yourself from their slavery. I get it. It's all you've known. Change is scary. You fear the unknown. You might be thinking, "Well, what if it doesn't work out?" or "What if nothing changes?" But did you ever stop to think, "What if it DOES?"

"What is life without all of my unnecessary baggage," you ask, right? It's a very liberated sense of being where you stop merely existing as a human, spirit-filled landfill. When you finally plow your way out of all of the debt, debris, disaster, and debacle of others that you were buried beneath, you can then begin living the meaningful, fruitful, abundantly fulfilling life that you were intended to have. Your life CAN be free of guilt, shame, blame, worry and pressure of pleasing others more than yourself.

In September 2015, I had to make some tough decisions about relocating from New York and moving back to Atlanta. I had lived in New York for nine months, and I knew and sensed with every fiber of my spirit being that I had done everything there that I needed to do at that time. Something was shifting. I had experienced enough change to know what it looks like when a door is closing. I no longer need to be forced out. I just willingly go and trust that my angels will support me as I go with the flow. I took a vacation to Daytona Beach to be with my nephew, Spencer, who was approaching his junior year of college. My sister, his mom, Phy, flew in from Chicago and we met there. As we spent time together, I mentioned that I sensed I should leave New York and that I didn't want anyone to think this or that, but I have to do what's best for me. Before I could continue, my sister interjected with sound wisdom and said, "Stop right there! Did you hear what you said? You have to do what's best for YOU and that's all that matters. You can put the period right there."

See, my old pattern of thinking almost crept up on me. But my sister, who is one of my greatest supporters and spiritual guides, has seen my journey to become myself and she could remind me of what I had adopted as a new thought pattern. The useless thoughts about "What will people think?" "Will they approve?" or "What will they say?" are no longer relevant. Those thoughts have been replaced with new thoughts that say, "I have to do what's best for me." After that experience, I decided to rid myself of another old pattern, which was the need to explain or justify my decisions.

As I boxed up my things in New York in preparation to go to Atlanta, I could hear the echoes of presumptuous conversations and disapproving tones. Nevertheless, I knew within myself that moving was the best thing for me and that all things were new! I had a renewed sense of self. My spirit was renewed. My mind was renewed. My body was renewed. My voice was renewed. My marriage was renewed. I had no plans to apologize, explain, or justify it. I said to myself, "It just is...so let it be."

When my mom got an unction that I was headed back South, she called and said, "Nadia, I have a question for you, and you can tell me it's none of my business, but what made you decide to leave New York? I thought you said you weren't coming back this way?"

I said, "Oh that's not complicated at all. It's actually very simple--it's because I wanted to."

I went on to tell her how much I respect her as my mother and I know she's just being a good parent by showing concern. I shared with her that I will always tell her when I've made a decision, but by no means will I explain it or justify it--not even to my own mama.

I learned that doing what's best for you is something you never need approval for! Now, it will take time to transform your mind into the clear space that houses new truths, such as, "I'm worth it!" "I deserve it!" "I am enough!" or "I must do what's best for me without approval." However, if you rehearse the truth as much as you have rehearsed the lies, then a new, more empowering pattern starts to form. But it begins with you letting go of the weight you've carried and the lies that have only thwarted your progress. If you can transform your mind, you can transform your entire being. You can radically shift how you think, speak, eat, live, pray, work, strategize, create, react, decide, choose, respond, and interact with others.

Ever growing,

Nadia

TODAY'S THOUGHT

You can change whenever you are ready. Trust yourself. NEVER apologize for choosing YOU!

TODAY'S TRANSFORMATION JOURNAL

Today, I found it challenging to transform my thoughts when

_____

_____

_____

_____

Today, I found it easy to transform my thoughts when

_____

_____

_____

_____

The key thought from Today's Chronicle I will focus on is

_____

_____

_____

_____

Legacy Chronicle, No. 3: Your Name Is Your Integrity

Every day, think as you wake up, 'today I am fortunate to be alive, I have a precious human life, I am not going to waste it. I am going to use all my energies to develop myself to expand my heart out to others, to achieve enlightenment for the benefit of all beings. I am going to have kind thoughts towards others, I am not going to get angry or think badly about others. I am going to benefit others as much as I can.

— HIS HOLINESS THE 14TH DALAI LAMA

TODAY'S CHRONICLE FROM NADIA

Dear You,

ave your parents or grandparents ever told you "your name is all you've got"? If so, that was likely your first teaching on integrity. They usually share this statement as either a warning before you jeopardize your character or just after you did something to put your character in question. My mom would add to that teaching an admonishment about how good manners and respect would take you further than any amount of money or fame. These lessons about character are what help me keep my name in tact and my ego tamed.

Sure, I like to dress nicely, ride in luxury, enjoy fine dining, smell like expensive perfumes, and live posh. But who doesn't? However, to what extent will one go to attain and maintain a lavish lifestyle? Truth be told, I experience a prosperous life on a conservative budget. I'm not financially rich, yet. But my life is full and abundant in all of the resources I need to do as I desire with ease and effortlessness. I am not lacking in any way. However, I don't pretend to be someone I'm not, I don't "Rob Peter to pay Paul." I give much to others out of the blessed life I live, and I make an honest living. I'm not flashy, I don't boast, I don't brag, and I don't look down on anyone just because I may appear to be in a somewhat better position than them. I don't steal, kill, or rob to live my life. I live according to what I believe and manifest. Most importantly, whether I'm in just enough or plenty, I treat people fairly and lovingly. How

I regard others is not based on what materials or accolades I have attained because those things are all fleeting. These are the kind of decisions that help to formulate a person's character. It's the behaviors you enact when people are and, more importantly, aren't watching. That is what matters in the grander scheme of things. It's how well you live your life while on the Earth, the contributions you've made that shape your legacy and how well that legacy will speak of you when you you're no longer here to speak for yourself.

What happens when you transition from this life? What will people say about you? Will they exclaim about how much money you had, what cars you drove, the fine linens you wore, the lies you told, how you helped no one, how you cheated others, or how you stole the work of others to make your own name great? Will they say what a humanitarian you were, how honest you were, how diligently you worked, how you constantly evolved, how you hailed the needs of others as great as your own, how you served the less fortunate, or how you facilitated healing for the downtrodden? Will they say that you reached out to the lost, had a heart of gold, never looked down on others, shared your wealth and success, made them laugh in hard times, let them cry in sad times, listened when no one else would, and was a positive force to be reckoned with?

What is the story of YOUR name?

With Integrity,

Nadia

TODAY'S THOUGHT

The choice is yours! How you live is how you'll be remembered. Be mindful of what you say, how you treat others, and how you cheat others! Your name is all you have!

TODAY'S INTEGRITY JOURNAL

Today, I found it challenging to stay in integrity when

_____

_____

_____

_____

Today, I found it easy to stay in integrity when

_____

_____

_____

_____

The key thought from Today's Chronicle I will focus on is

_____

_____

_____

_____

Legacy Chronicle, No. 4: What Harvest Looks Like

Before the fruits of prosperity can come, the storms of life need to first bring the required rains of testing, which mixes with the seeds of wisdom to produce a mature harvest.

— LINCOLN PATZ

TODAY'S CHRONICLE FROM NADIA

Dear Farmer Friends,

If you're human, you have a natural inclination to imagine what your harvest should look like. This notion comes from what you KNOW you sowed. We even look at seeds that our counterparts have sown that look similar to ours, and we take note of their abundant harvest. That awareness increases our confidence that we will have the same awesome harvest. What we typically aren't privy to is the tremendous toiling, plowing, pruning, irrigating, and waiting that it took to produce their harvest. That is called the process. This is the part we aren't fond of but we need in order to get that amazing harvest. So, then the question arises: "What exactly SHOULD my harvest look like?" Well, that will all depend on your process.   One thing I don't like to partake in is out-of-season or un-ripened fruit. Overripe fruit can be mushy, while under ripe fruit can be bitter. Either way, it can be a total disappointment to your taste buds. Moreover, ingesting fruit that isn't done processing or that is beyond the ripening process will affect your digestive system and leave your belly writhed with pain and discomfort.

When you get a fruit that isn't perfectly ripe, you can bet your bottom dollar that something went awry in the PROCESS. Chances are the fruit reached the store in an un-ripened state and wasn't ready for consumption, or it arrived, was ready for immediate consumption, and had a limited shelf life. There's also a possibility that the farmer's tending practices may have impacted the outcome of the harvest. Whatever the case, the fruit didn't mature the way it should have in order for it to be in its most enjoyable state. Now compare that experience to the juicy, sweet fruit of the farmer who went through the proper process to get the desired results. Consider how different of an experience you had with the fruit once you better understood its proper season and what it should look and taste like when it's done processing. It's delectable, right?

I definitely love the way the results of patience taste. I am ever aware that abundance is all around me and wants to flow to me with ease and effortlessness. With that in mind, I still respect the process of arriving at that knowing-ness.   The truth is NO ONE knows exactly what their harvest will look like or even what the Universe will send your way so that you can get what you sowed for. Everybody wants the fruit, but hardly anybody wants to endure the tediousness of plucking, pruning, or weathering a storm. Who really says to themselves, "I'm so excited about this storm coming because I know the sun is coming out next"?

In this season of my life, I'm on the brink of a harvest greater than I could ever anticipate. It's also tremendously challenging to accept that I had to release what I thought was already BIG to gain BIGGER. I realized that I had to let go of something precious to make room for something more valuable. I recognized that I had to face the ugly truths about myself to arrive at the beauty that I am. I had to endure severe rains to get a mature harvest.

Now this isn't how I pictured my harvest coming at all. Nevertheless, it is here. Although the rain is falling at a monsoon rate, I see a rainbow, which means that no matter how cloudy it appears to be, the Sun is near. No matter what, I respect the process. The truth is that Abundance is all around me!

Abundantly,

Nadia

(In honor of the legacy of G. DeWayne Wallace)

TODAY'S THOUGHT

I am not sent here to hustle, grind, struggle, or suffer! Abundance is all around me and it flows to me easily and effortlessly. I sow well that I may reap well. Regardless of my process, I am grateful and I am worthy of a beautiful harvest!

TODAY'S PREPARING FOR THE HARVEST JOURNAL

Today, I found it challenging to prepare and accept my harvest when_____

_____

_____

_____

Today, I found it easy to prepare and accept my harvest when

_____

_____

_____

_____

The key thought from Today's Chronicle I will focus on is

_____

_____

_____

_____

Legacy Chronicle, No. 5.: Grace To Be Me!

TODAY'S CHRONICLE FROM NADIA

Dear You,

It wasn't that long ago that I became comfortable in the skin I'm in. I had no idea that I had been a people-pleaser for most of my life. I discovered that I had been doing what was expected of me and that my high expectations of myself were simply the standards that I allowed others to impose on me. Whether intentional or unintentional, these family, career, religious, and relationship standards were imposed. Let's face it: I was MISERABLE! Although I met everyone's approval, I wasn't able to be ME! I hadn't ever really stopped and surveyed myself by asking questions such as,

"Who are you REALLY?

What do YOU want?

What is YOUR vision for yourself?

"How do YOU feel about your relationship with this specific person?"

I don't think I knew I COULD ask those questions. Once I started to taste liberty, the bonds of popular standards and opinions started to loosen. But if freedom got murky for me, I'd just resort to the familiar. I'd run towards the things I assuredly knew. Liberty was scary! It meant I'd actually have to create my own standards and get to know myself better.

I faced my fear of being different from everyone else and being OK with being so uniquely different. Being a standard, mediocre, average, or "go along to get along" girl is just not who I am or have ever been.

How did I do it? I got downright frustrated! I cried out to (more like screamed at) The One who created and carefully designed me. I said, "Listen now, God. I've been praying to you for a long time and I need to know why you won't change me? Why won't you make me more likable? Why did you make me so different? Why won't you take this or that away from me so I measure up?"

I was acting as if God was outside of me and like I was separate from the Source Energy that created me like itself. Trying to be anything other than who I was created to be definitely had me feeling separate from my truest Self. I was feeling small, stressed, overwhelmed, and exhausted. Eventually, I cried a cry of surrender. I was tired of not feeling absolutely sure. I remember that I started saying "Yes" in a low mumble that rumbled, rattled and vibrated on the inside of me. I was home alone. I felt a little weird at first having this encounter where it was eerily quiet in the house and all I could hear was my internal voice that started to become audible as my own voice.

So I kept saying yes aloud but quietly. But my soul was calling for a real release...a sincere letting go...an honest "Yes." I kept feeling that internal nudge and tugging, "Just say yes! Just let go! Trust me! Say yes!" I started to feel like there was no other choice and I was almost annoyed like "OK, OK, OK...I'll say yes!"

And all of a sudden the "yes" effervesced, bubbled all the way up, and came out as a resounding sound!! I screamed "YESSS!!! YESSS!! YESSS!!" to the top of my lungs and my soul began to cleanse itself with my tears. I cried even more. I didn't know what was next after the yes. What was the plan? Where do I go from here? I became still. The clarity came. Right there in the stillness, the Spirit of Love met me when I was willing to be undone, uninhibited, real, and honest! I had said yes to God, my calling, and my purpose many times before. However, it was more from a learned behavior kind of space that was as sincere as it could possibly be based on my limited understanding.

But this time was different. I was choosing to connect to my truest Self without pretense or expectation from another person. I just wanted to take my own divine path as my authentic Self. I wanted to show up in the world better, more real, and ultimately free! And right there in that moment where I let go of everything I thought I was and everything I thought I knew as true...God was most present. I met Unconditional Love. Sweetly, gently, and delicately, the Spirit of Love reassured me that I was made perfectly, created as a whole being, and had free access to an unending supply of love that flows parallel to a river of grace that had always been there. God let me know that there would always be enough love and grace that would be sufficient enough for all I am and all I am not. My Higher Self let me know that nothing about me catches It off guard. Where I am weak, It is ALL power. Where I'm human and flawed, Its grace abounds much more. And I was clear that I didn't need to "try" anymore—I could just BE and that is more than enough.

Loving you the way you are,

TODAY'S THOUGHT

Today, I'm being Me and living in the grace of God that allows me to just be who I am—unapologetically!

TODAY'S GRACE JOURNAL

Today, I found it challenging to accept grace when

_____

_____

_____

_____

Today, I found it easy to accept grace when

_____

_____

_____

_____

The key thought from Today's Chronicle I will focus on is

_____

_____

_____

_____

Legacy Chronicle, No. 6: Got Light?

TODAY'S CHRONICLE FROM NADIA

Dear Light Being,

I love meeting people on neutral ground and having the opportunity to dialogue with them on a non-threatening, non-intimidating, and non-judgmental turf. When people feel they are in a safety zone they will be completely open and honest with you! And guess what? I found out that sometimes Christians do a horrible job representing the heart of Christ. Muslims sometimes do a poor job emulating the ways of the prophet Muhammad and the deen as outlined in the Quran. Some Buddhists misrepresent the original intent of Gautama Buddha. Some Jews, who practice Judaism, miscommunicate the authenticity of their father Abraham with their staunchness. There are followers of Confucius that have deviated from his teachings in the Analects that encourage the virtuous practices of "jen" and "li".

You get the picture.

Sometimes when it comes to our various beliefs systems, we're more like religious tyrants who have a monopoly on God. We act as members of a secret faith society that you have to be perfect, privileged, or spiritually mature enough to be inducted into. We're not champions for The Spirit as much as we are cheerleaders for our churches, mosques, temples, and masjids and publicists for our religious leaders. Far too often our only response to people's problems when we perceive that they are void of a higher power is "You should come to my church Sunday," "You can take the shahada during Ramadan," "Let me invite you to a meditation," or "Let me introduce you to the Torah." Huh?!?! You mean you invite them to a building or to a set of practices because you just believe that your church, pastor, leader, or belief system are magical and you neglect to give them an invitation to God? News flash: inviting people to our religious culture isn't discipleship.

Think of it this way--would it make sense to you if you went to a noted mechanic who lives minutes away and has all of the knowledge, tools, and skills he needs to fix your vehicle; however, instead of giving you the service you are confident he can provide, he gives you directions to where he works an hour away and assures you he can fix it there. He then leaves you vulnerable to take the risk that your car could break down on the way. That is senseless, right?

Some people that you encounter are never going to come to your religious facility or adopt your practices. Then what? Are they just a lost cause? NO! You have everything inside of you that they need to find the light to their own path. That's why they were sent to YOU! You don't send them away in hopes that someone else will do the job. YOUR light drew them to YOU! Invite them to the Most High by the way you treat them on their journey by allowing God to be demonstrated THROUGH YOU.

Understand that God is not happening OUTSIDE of you; God is happening AS you! We feel more confident preaching, singing, prophesying, and laying hands on the same people every week who are already apart of our fold and should already have "the light." We keep taking our light into places that are already lit. But what about people who are in the dark about who the Spirit of Love really is? Do we just keep hoarding all the rights to Christ, Muhammad, Buddha, and the Abrahamic promises and acting like we have a monopoly on God?

Wisdom and Knowledge are light. Ignorance is darkness.

Man has managed to organize religion in such a way that it deifies the leader and minimizes the Source of Light. Obedience to rules that are handed down to the followers has taken precedence over empowering these beings with the truth that they are a reflection of the Spirit of Love. But as opposed to making that rich deposit into the hearts of man, more often the followers of each religion receive scorn, rebuke, and judgment if they don't "follow the rules." Can you imagine how depressing and stressful of an existence that is to believe that the Spirit of Love has designed the human experience to be filled with damnation, condemnation, and fear? No wonder it's hard to exhibit something towards others that you aren't receiving.

There's no doubt that religion can get a tad bit confusing. But the way I see it is that inside of each these structured organizations are several sub-organizations who adopt various schools of thought and individual truths. Then people who are either born into that sect or have been introduced to it will gravitate to the religious culture that resonates with them. That would mean there is no "cookie cutter" way of practicing that religion because the parishioners inside of each organization don't even share the same perspective on tenants and doctrine. Let's take Christianity, for example. Within Christianity there are innumerable denominations or sub-organizations. In every denomination there are varied cultural practices, disciplines, doctrines, and teachings. If you venture outside of the U.S., that will add an entirely different category of cultural religious diversity for the same religion. If that is the case, wherein lies the need for rigidity and judgment? Why judge someone based on YOUR perspective and experience? Why not just maturely dialogue with them about their perspective and experience and you share your perspective and experience? If for some reason you still find it necessary to judge them, you can at least do so fairly by basing your measure on whether they are living by their own convictions, tenants, doctrines and truths, and not YOURS!

In my Christian upbringing and experience, I learned that people of other faiths sometimes don't know the truth of Christ because most Christians don't know it. What I've often observed is that many people know all the mechanics of their religion; however these formalities keep out the authentic experience of connecting with the divine Source of Love. Let's face it--the pious approach isn't attractive, but love is! Sometimes we're so gung-ho about all of the particulars that we end up portraying ourselves as mean, demanding, and self-righteous title wearers. Instead of fighting for position or recognition, we should be eager to serve. Mahatma Gandhi once said, "I like your Christ...I don't like your Christians...Your Christians are so unlike your Christ." This statement, at its core, can be applied to any religious faith. No matter what faith you practice or what school of thought you subscribe to, BE the light! The light is not tucked away at your spiritual center—it's in YOU. You ARE the light and you're here to keep your light on to remind others of the light they are so they can turn theirs on, too. Keep your spiritual wattage high so you can do you part in helping illuminate darkness. You ARE the light of the world!

Love and Light,

Nadia

THOUGHT FOR TODAY

This is my simple religion. There is no need for temples; no need for complicated philosophy. Our own brain, our own heart is our temple; the philosophy is kindness.

—DALAI LAMA

TODAY'S BECOMING A LIGHT JOURNAL

Today, I found it challenging to be a light when

_____

_____

_____

_____

Today, I found it easy to be a light when

_____

_____

_____

_____

The key thought from Today's Chronicle I will focus on is

_____

_____

_____

_____

Legacy Chronicle, No.7: Sowing And Reaping

Hey My Bountiful Beauty,

Be not deceived—you will reap what you sow! Whatever you feed will grow! Most things that materialize happen in the mind first. We can actually think a thing into existence. If you think negative thoughts, you will unconsciously attract negativity to you!   The same is true for the positive. You can create a positive world by what you think, speak, believe, see, do, and allow to keep you company!

Some of us volunteer ourselves to be deceived because of how we condition ourselves to think. What makes us think we can steal from others, lie about them, cheat on our significant others, preach one gospel and live another separate life, rape, molest, or abuse people, have scandalous affairs, racketeer, sell stolen products, bamboozle, and swindle people and never see it come back to us in some form? We think we can sow but not reap? What a joke!

The Bible calls that very thought process deception! How dare you think that you're so VIP that The Universe will ignore your seeds? How can you be so misguided as to reason that Karma will repay you good when you sowed the opposite? Can you sow lemon seeds and get a crop of pomegranates? NO! To think as much would be to ultimately deceive yourself while thinking you're fooling Spirit and everyone else!

In the classic movie "The Color Purple," the lead character, Celie, plainly states this principle as follows—"Everything you done to me, already done to you." There's no way that we can move through life believing that our actions do not have consequences. The results of your actions may not show up today, but trust and believe that it is ALL coming back to you. That is why is it imperative that we stand guard at the gates our minds—and our mouths!

Whether you regard the truth principle as "What goes around comes around," or "You reap what you sow," either way you slice it, the lesson is the same. Don't trick yourself into believing there are no consequences for your actions.

With great joy,

Nadia

TODAY'S THOUGHT

If you've done nothing good,
expect nothing good!

TODAY'S SOWING AND REAPING JOURNAL

Today, I found it challenging to step into sowing and reaping

in my life when_____

_____

_____

_____

Today, I found it easy to step into sowing and reaping in my

life when_____

_____

_____

_____

The key thought from Today's Chronicle I will focus on is

_____

_____

_____

_____

Legacy Chronicle, No. 8: Death: It Is Not Final

TODAY'S CHRONICLE FROM NADIA

Dear Energetic Being,

Death is an inevitable, unavoidable mystery. In death, we have no certainty except that it must take place. James 4:14 (in The Amplified Bible) reads, "Yet you do not know [the least thing] about what may happen tomorrow. What is the nature of your life? You are [really] but a wisp of vapor (a puff of smoke, a mist) that is visible for a little while and then disappears [into thin air]."

For some people, death seems like an end with no hope. You could be right. Death could be the end for you. However, that all depends on what you choose to believe and, ultimately, how you are choosing to spend your life. I have made a conscious choice to not be hopeless and to live my life on purpose! I now understand that it's not really about what path you choose as much as it's about what you choose to do on your path.

We all have a specific set of gifts to fulfill the purpose for which we were sent here in the Earth. The adjacent reality to that is when you have wholeheartedly acknowledged and fulfilled that purpose, your body will return to the Earth and your soul will release itself as the energy it is. If you spent your time in the earth building a legacy that changed lives, the spirit of your heart, your work, and your commitment will outlive you for ages to come!

Take into consideration the life and legacy of Dr. King, Harriet Tubman, Malcolm X, Sojourner Truth, Bob Marley, Mahatma Gandhi, Nelson Mandela, Mother Theresa, Maya Angelou, Mary McLeod Bethune, Dr. Sebi, Marcus Garvey, Jesus Christ, and Muhammad. Their work was great and their missions were tedious. They understood their assignment in the Earth. They came. They answered the call. They impacted us. They conquered. They transitioned. They live on! Everyone wants to be remembered and not considered a mere mist. But what will you be remembered FOR? And what are you doing about it NOW?

I used to be afraid to die until I realized that it only made me afraid to LIVE! I don't know about you, but I know my purpose in the Earth and I can't expend valuable energy being afraid that I will run out of "time" to do it. Time is one of the greatest illusions ever! When I have completed my work, I will gladly transition out of this soul clothing, return to the free flowing energy I began as, and let my legacy of love, compassion, and service to all of mankind live on. Ultimately, I'd like for my higher self to be pleased with me in that I Am a reflection of its Love and that I've accomplished all that I agreed to do in this lifetime.

I don't like to think about death and I don't like morbid talk. (And this isn't some eerie farewell letter because I'm clear that I've far more life to live and works to accomplish!) But it's a conversation we like to avoid and fear having. Admittedly, it used to shake me to my core. However, it's a reality and I want to help you face it with purpose. Use your energy here in the physical realm wisely and focus on allowing yourself to be impactful, not impressive. When it comes down to it, in the final analysis of my life all I can say is may every life I've touched return the favor to some other life. May the legacy I create live beyond me. May the love I've shared transcend time and space. May the works I've done speak for me!

Lovingly,

Nadia

TODAY'S THOUGHT

Death is never final when you have done your work on purpose!

You will LIVE ON!!

TODAY'S LIVING LIFE JOURNAL

Today, I found it challenging to reject the fear of death when

_____

_____

_____

_____

Today, I found it easy to reject the fear of death when

_____

_____

_____

_____

The key thought from Today's Chronicle I will focus on is

_____

_____

_____

_____

Legacy Chronicle, No. 9: The Power To Say No

TODAY'S CHRONICLE FROM NADIA

Dear You,

I never considered myself a "Yes" person but I've said "Yes" more often than I would have liked. In retrospect, it was likely because I thought it was the "right thing to do." But why? Many reasons, I suppose. I didn't want to disappoint anyone. I didn't want to let anyone down. I didn't want to ruffle any feathers. I wanted to be deemed dependable. I didn't want to cause a kerfuffle and make waves in my family structure. So my "Yes" in quite a few instances meant I didn't do what was best for ME. I didn't use my voice. I didn't stick up for myself. I didn't honor myself. I didn't defend myself. I didn't advocate for me. I didn't know my own power. So, I sometimes suffered in silence.

I recall the first time I exercised my "No," and realized its power. I was twelve years old. That fateful day when I came home from school, my babysitter awaited my arrival. The usual "encounter" ensued. The only unusual thing was this time, I said, "NO!" It was a timorous, somewhat uncommitted "No," but it was a "No" nonetheless. Although I rehearsed this day in my mind on many occasions, I didn't know I was going to pick that day to go through with it. I remember being ready to retract my "No," afraid that I had offended my "offender." Just before I could immerse myself in second-guessing and the guilt of rejecting the non-consensual act, she asked me "Why you saying 'No'? You don't want to?" As if I EVER wanted to!

I readily responded with breathy exhaustion: "Because I don't want to. I'm tired of this." And in some rare miraculous moment it seemed, I wasn't forced to participate in something with her that I had never agreed to in the first place. I had found my voice for the first time.   I knew it would take some getting used to this newly realized power.

Not long after that incident, I got to practice my "No" again. This time, I was far more certain, vehement, unapologetic, and downright belligerent. As I lay across my mom's bed, I felt my cream-colored, red-trimmed teddy bear nightgown slowly rising. He had searched my mom's house and found me, while my mom and his mom sat on the porch sharing laughs. I lay there—still, frozen, almost playing possum, and waiting for the moment to exert my power. I gave no thought as to whether I would offend this particular offender. He had long since worn out his welcome. I bolted up! And with my power in high gear and full throttle, my "NO!" roared and I paired it with rapid pummeling! A gut wrenching "No" accompanied every punch and I never explained myself any further. My "No" was a complete sentence for the first time. I laid the silent "Yes" to rest.

I understand the power of "Yes" as well, surrendering to a process that is there to serve one's best interest. I understand that to give a "Yes" you must be present and aware of what you're agreeing to. Although I haven't always committed to it and gotten the "Yes" right in every life occurrence since I was twelve years old, those experiences laid a foundation on which I could continue to grow, build, understand, and practice my power. I renew my covenant with my "No" as often as I see fit. I don't discriminate—no one is exempt from my "No." I now understand the importance of choosing me, advocating for ME, rooting for ME, investing in ME, nurturing ME, and simply loving me FIRST, without explanation or apology, without guilt or regret. Others may need me, but I need me MORE! I can only be as good to others as I Am to myself.

Any time saying "Yes" to anyone or anything will mean "No" for my best interest and overall well-being, I will graciously say "No." My "No" to you is my "Yes" to me! And I don't feel guilty about it.

Love and Light,

TODAY'S THOUGHT

No one typically asks for an explanation when you answer with a "Yes," so don't offer an explanation when you answer with a "No." Stand in your power to refuse anything that causes you to deprive yourself of you.

Today's POWER OF NO Journal

Today, I found it challenging to say no when

_____

_____

_____

_____

Today, I found it easy to say no when

_____

_____

_____

_____

The key thought from Today's Chronicle I will focus on is

_____

_____

_____

_____

EPILOGUE

THE FREE THAT IS YOU

TODAY'S FINAL LETTER FROM NADIA

My Dearest Loves,

We are so often weighted down by standards created by society, traditions we are born into and thoughts, ideals, perspectives imposed on us from our first breath. It can feel like we are shackled by customary rules just because "They said so," and there are no signs of freedom anywhere. More often than not, we are blindly stricken with mental slavery and we become comfortable with being told what, when, and how to do it, despite the fact that no one can answer the "Why?" of it all. Most of the time, we never even question "Why" our liberty has been taken in this "free" world. Even with love being the most free-spirited power there is, we're told who we should love and we are expected to follow the traditions thereof. But has anyone ever stopped to ask, "Why?"

My mom often tells the story of me being her "Why" child. She said you couldn't just TELL me to do something and think that was enough. I always needed an explanation to make sense of it all. A simple "because I said so" wouldn't suffice because then I'd need to know WHY you said so! Today I'm that same inquisitive, free spirit that some may perceive as a rebel of sorts. In my experience, any time another being can think independently of others or be liberated in his or her thinking, they will be deemed a rebel. I prefer to call myself FREE! What's the point of having my own mind if I'm going to let others dictate to me what to think? Isn't that what MY mind is for? I have no use for chains, boxes, small cramped mental spaces, antiquated ideals, unsupported opinions, outdated traditions, uneducated religious views, political mumbo-jumbo or any other imprisoning way of thinking.

I haven't always been totally free, but I have awakened from the dark controlling forces that once held my being-ness captive. I was that girl who said and did everything people expected of me. I sang, clapped, danced, preached, prayed, and spoke in tongues on cue. I attended every church service, conference, convocation, and prayer service. I stood in every offering line. I dated the guys others approved of or didn't date the ones who weren't approved of. I didn't consume adult beverages. I worked the 9-to-5 job. I never relocated outside of my home state to give myself a shot at my dreams. I danced to everyone's drum beat and couldn't figure out why I was still miserable after dotting every "i" and crossing every "t."

I was miserable because I wasn't at liberty to be my idea of ME! When I finally realized that, I started becoming my own best self and quite frankly, I'm enjoying getting to know myself. It is a very freeing experience! I learned that there is a difference between being and doing. My loves, you have to be alert, aware, clear, and sober-minded so that your "doings" are not fueled by the expectations of others, which in turn leaves your proverbial "tank" on empty. When you focus on "being," you stay present to the moment and you are ultimately grateful for who you are and what you have NOW!

If what you are doing doesn't align with who you really are, then you're not being yourself. This could mean that you don't think that being yourself is enough. If that is the case, then there is more internal work for you to do. The truth is that if people don't like who you're being when you're not doing as they please and if pleasing them is what matters most to you, you'll forever be doing what isn't true to your being.

NADIA'S FREEDOM COMMANDMENTS

Today, I encourage you to search yourself. Find out what you like. Indulge in what you discover about yourself along the way, but strike a balance. Laugh often with yourself. Travel when you want. Go shopping alone. Cry about things that matter to you. Date yourself. Write down your thoughts. Love freely. Pray as often as it hits you. Sing out loud. Dance until you sweat. Have a girls' night out or a guys' gathering and talk about everything under the sun. Do something you've never done. Go someplace you've never been. Run naked on a nude beach while flying a kite. Date and fall in love with that person who is taboo to everyone else. Be that rebel. Take the day off to chase butterflies and run through a field of lavender. Shave your head. Color your hair like the rainbow. Dance in the street. Move to another country. Say "No" to others when it means saying "Yes" to you. Say something you've always wanted to say. Be YOU. Be FREE!

Remember, YOU ARE MORE THAN ENOUGH in the ease of BEING than you'll ever be in the race of DOING!

You are what your deepest desire is...

As is your desire, so is your intention...

As is your intention, so is your will...

As is your will, so is your deed...

As is your deed, so is your destiny!"

-Teaching of the Hindu Upanishads

Footloose and fancy-free,

Nadia

TODAY'S THOUGHT

Desire Deeply. Dream BIG. Follow the path of your destiny, unapologetically. Free your mind, let go, and just BE!

CREATING YOUR NEXT CHRONICLE

Close your eyes and look 10 years into the future.

What do you see?

Write a description of what you WILL BE and what your life WILL BE like in the next decade. Create this vision in bright, bold, vivid, and beautiful color. Imagine operating fully in your purpose, standing fully in your power, and accepting all the love your heart can stand—AND BEYOND!

_____

_____

_____

_____

_____

_____

_____

_____

_____

Acknowledgements

Good, you are indeed the Great "I AM." You are the Infinitely Loving Presence that allows me to live, move, and have my very being. Mother-Father God, you have guided me within to You, to the Center of All Being, to self-love, to healing, to wholeness, to your endless goodness. I am so grateful to know that you and I are one and we're never separate. Thank you for directing my path to this now moment. I am here now. I am free now. I am abundant now. I am joyous now and I am grateful now. Thank you to the God within me.

To my editor, Leah Lakins¬¬—You are the thread that pulled this whole manuscript together to structure it into a complete book. Thank you for honoring my ideas, my thoughts, my heart and making it all make sense. I've known since I was in middle school that I was a writer and I knew that I wanted to write a book. Thank you for helping make that little girl's dream come true. You are the definition of God-send. Thank you, my friend!

To my Mom, Wilodean Perry¬¬—What an incredible being you are! What a powerful woman you are. What a superpower you are. Your entire life has been an inspiration to me. Your words of wisdom have been my meat when even physical food couldn't satisfy me.Your very existence is so strong, graceful, intuitive, peaceable, giving, and unconditionally loving. As I observe you, understand you, listen to you, and accept your gentle guidance and reassurance, I know that I can do ANYTHING. You spoke to my greatness long before I could actually see it. You would always intuitively say, "You're gonna be on the big screen." Thank you for seeing me, Mama, in ways that I couldn't see myself.

Your powerful prayer life has been one of my life's most priceless treasures, inspiring me and teaching me to be fervent in prayer. I have watched you serve everyone and everything without ever complaining. It's because of you I know how to compassionately serve others . I am so thankful to have you as one of my most favorite intercessors in prayer, as my Earth, as my best friend and confidant, as my guide, as my safe place, as my example of unconditional love, as my teacher of independence, as my "Chocolate Drop," as my greatest support, and as the greatest mother I could ever have. Thank you, Mama, for being here and encouraging me, reminding me to stay focused, and letting me know you're proud of me every step of the way. I love you endlessly!

To my one and only sister, T. Phyllisia Taylor—Thank you for being one of my greatest spiritual guides, prayer partners, reflections, and soulmates EVER. You helped to awaken me to so much truth and enlightenment and I always enjoy being your student. Thank you for praying for a sister so that God would send me to you. Now you have your own personal unicorn (LOL!).You've been my "A1 since day one" and I wouldn't be who I am without you. I Love You with my WHOLE heart, Sissy-pooh, and I'm grateful for all of the ways you love and support me.

To my brothers Tolliver and Darious Perry—Thank you for being a constant source of love, loyalty, and support in my life. Tee, thank you for listening to me, hearing what I didn't say and reminding me to "work on your lean," that it's OK to ask for help and to remember that my support system WANTS to help me. I'll always hold that moment dear—it changed my life. Sweet, thank you for always reassuring me whenever I say, "I just want to make you proud" that if I don't do another thing that you're already proud of me just as I am. You all keep me grounded and secure in the knowing that no matter where I go in this life, there are two tried and true soldiers who will always be down for me without question. I love you both with every fiber of my being!

To my Godmother, Earthia Jenkins—I learned from you how to love so freely and deeply till it's almost palpable. I learned from you the art of being an eternal student. You also showed me that the teacher can be the student because you've always been so willing to learn from me. You taught me how to pray the "word of God." You gave me the tools, you gave me spiritual food. Moreover, you loved me when I wasn't easy to love. Thank you Mommy, for being love personified and for letting me see and experience life through your loving lenses. Your love has helped to shape my love for humanity because it's God's Love. Thank you for helping me smooth out the rough edges and become a better being so that I could offer the world this wisdom in a way that is easy to receive. Thank you, Mommy, for helping me to "listen to my heart beat!" I love you infinitely!

To my Twin, John-Paul Moore—Where do I begin? You are such an incredible reflection of my soul and I am FOREVER grateful to DeWayne Wallace for making certain that I didn't miss out on the ultimate life blessing of being connected to one of the most beautiful souls this life can bring—YOU! You're always down to go the distance with me on my visions, desires, and dreams. No matter what I ask, you're always willing to avail yourself. Thank you for your commitment to pure excellence in helping me get this baby birthed out and for providing me with the most dynamic marketing and design team this world has to offer. You're such a gift and I'm honored and blessed to have you present with me as my own personal gift from God. I've learned that "gratitude brings abundance." I'm abundantly grateful for you. Thank you. I love you MUCHO!

To my Pastors, Greg Stamper and Yolanda Batts—I've said it to you before and I'll say it again, you two are the divine outpicturing of my most loving internal dialogue with Source. You have helped me to heal and rewrite my pastoral story. You all are REAL game changers. The two of you are just solid, beautiful beings and I couldn't be more honored to be serving with you all at Celebration Spiritual Center. You all are a balm to my soul and I'm SO glad that as I re-imagined being pastored that I left the "who" and the "how" to God. I could never have imagined that you two incredibly loving, brilliant, masterful light beings would be the answer to the "who" and "how." As always, God does all things well including you two. Thank you for availing yourselves as the beings that Spirit can move through to guide others to their wholeness, healing, calling, purpose, and highest joy.

Thank you for BEING Jesus, Buddha, Mohammed, Krishna... Yolanda and Greg, the Christ. Thank you for providing tools, sound wisdom, life-altering teachings, and a loving space for me to operate from my wholeness and be my calling. Thank you for seeing the Divine in me, as me, and through me. Thank you for reminding me that I'm sinless and that I'm perfect, whole, and complete just as God created me and that God will never change Its mind about Its perfect creation and good idea. Thank you for teaching me how to save own life. You all the eternal gifts of wisdom that just keep on giving. Thank you for committing to the calling. I love you both Infinitely, always and in ALL Ways!

To my Soulmie, Tamika Jackson, my "Bess-Dee," Deidre Etheredge, and my "Grace,"Antyon Wallace, and my Roomie, Nancy—You four have anchored me in pure love. You have seen me as undone as I could possibly be and you still never saw me as anything less than love. Over the last almost two years, you all have been my hiding place, the treasure chest of all of my most valuable moments, and the vault of all of my unmentionable issues. I have trusted you all with parts of me that no one else knows. I thank you all for being my safe place, for reminding me of who and whose I Am, and for never giving up on me or allowing me to give up when life was working through me to shift me higher.

When I shifted, you all shifted; you didn't get shook in the shift. Thank you for your loyalty, your unwavering love, your chest, your lap, your shoulder, your ear, your heart space, your counsel, your nudges, your support, your understanding, your prayers, your mirror, your reflection, your confidentiality, your laughter, your ridiculousness, tomfoolery, and craziment (LOL!), and for being some of the greatest students and teachers. You all are so willing to learn from me and expand the borders of your norm. You receive from me and you pour into me freely. You all are life to me and I love you immeasurably and I'm SO blessed and so grateful to have you all doing life with me. Thank you for staying the course. We made it, my loves!

To Nia, Skyy, Ana, Genesis, Ava and Phy, my Leading Ladies Network tribe—I couldn't have done this without you all. We built a platform to blog and write, and it awakened the writer in me. You all trusted my guidance and leadership and it all culminated in this moment. Thank you for supporting me and trusting me every step of the way. I love you all with everything that I Am. Now besides Ana, who got next on the book writing?

To my AAP ELA teacher from W.G. Sanders Middle School, Mrs. Virginia Sanderson, my AP Honors English teachers from W.J. Keenan High School, Mrs. Betty Dicks and Mrs. Cindy Ryan, and my Public Speaking and Oral Interpretation professor from the College of Charleston, Dr. Shirley Moore—Thank you for teaching me the art of writing and communication, for gifting me the love for this craft, and for challenging me to abandon mediocrity and ascend to excellence. I hope I make you proud!

To my brother, my love, my most beloved Lance—I dedicate this book to your memory. You have been one of the greatest teachers of my life and by far the unsurpassed partner of my life. My light is that much brighter because of you. Thank you for allowing me to continue to be your light in the Earth and for being my chiefest of angels, orchestrating some of the most divine outcomes on my path like only you can. "... and the world shall know your name, recognize you came and changed the way my life has grown...and I'll never be the same. I'll carry on your legacy; your character inspires me...and though you had to leave, you will always be the greatest part of me." I love you "Boogie" in this life and beyond...for eternity.

Made in the USA
Columbia, SC
30 September 2020